Dec.

To Jim

Enjoy!

Roger E. Dow

The Practical Fly Tier

The Practical Fly Tier

No-Nonsense Patterns and Techniques
for Wet and Dry Flies, Nymphs, and Streamers

by Royce Dam

Compiled and composed by Mark Van Patten

Photography by Thom Beck

Edited by Art Scheck

STACKPOLE
BOOKS

Published by
STACKPOLE BOOKS
5067 Ritter Road
Mechanicsburg, PA 17055
www.stackpolebooks.com

Printed in China

10 9 8 7 6 5 4 3 2 1

Library of Congress Cataloging-in-Publication Data

CIP data on file with Library of Congress

ISBN 0-8117-1027-0

Royce Dam has tied at every Federation of Fly Fishers (FFF) International Conclave since 1983. He has taught fly tying in China, Bhutan, and more than fifteen states, and has twice attended Fly Fair in Holland. Royce has donated many framed fly plates as auction items for fund-raising events. The flies in these plates range from classic salmon flies to patterns for all types of lake, stream, and ocean fishing. Royce has received many awards for his fly-tying abilities and support of the mission of the FFF, including Friend of the Southern Council FFF (1988) and Contributing Artisan Achievement Award, Great Lakes Council FFF (1992). He is also a recipient of the Federation of Fly Fishers annual "Buz" Buszek Memorial Fly-Tying Award (1994).

Royce brings a new look at an ancient art form. He has discovered pragmatic approaches and more efficient ways to achieve fly-tying perfection. More than once, as you learn from this master, you will slap your forehead and mutter, "I can't believe how easy this is."

This is not a pattern book. The patterns in this book were chosen to teach you certain techniques. Of course, Royce uses some of his favorite patterns, and it couldn't hurt to try a few in your home waters. Each section of the manual progresses to the next. If you follow the system, section by section, your fly-tying speed and quality will improve. Royce blends basic information on tools and techniques with more complex methodologies to appeal to both the novice and the most advanced tier.

—Mark Van Patten

CONTENTS

FOREWORD

It's strange how a river can have such a strong effect on the development of fly tiers. In all cases, there has been a challenge offered by the river that requires a level of artistry and imagination in the patterns developed to fish it. The flies of Marinaro were prompted by the pastoral Letort Spring Creek, George Grant developed his magical skills of weaving hair hackles to match the conditions he encountered on the Big Hole, and the No-Hackle flies of Swisher and Richards developed from observations made during a *Pseudocloeon* hatch on Michigan's Au Sable River.

Wisconsin's Wolf River has also influenced the tying tactics of many. While their tying styles remain their own, they have all undergone a convergent evolution in fly dressing. This homogeneity of style was not developed so much by collaboration as it was forced upon them by the river itself. Big, brawling, and demanding, the Wolf does not coddle its trout or its insects, and imitations had better be as broad-shouldered as the naturals they purport to mimic. And as long as the river flows peat-brown through the conifers and northern hardwoods of the highlands of Wisconsin, as long as it tumbles and dances over the glacial debris dumped there 12,000 years ago, as long as its creatures continue their annual rites of life and death, skilled artisans like Royce Dam will draw their creative strength from it.

Royce Dam lives in Wauwatosa, just outside Milwaukee. For most of his working life, he operated an 8,000-pound, steam-powered hammer forge, making camshafts, gear blanks, and other metal forgings. It was hot, heavy work, and Royce's massive, powerful hands and forearms reflect his one-time vocation. Split fingernails, cuts, bruises, and coarse skin were also a part of the job. With his blemishes and fingers the size of bratwursts, Royce seems an unlikely candidate for fly tying. Nonetheless, he is a superb and innovative tier.

Royce began tying flies to fish for bluegills and other warmwater species when he was in his twenties. In the early 1950s Royce and three of his friends began tying professionally. Royce specialized in chenille-bodied patterns for panfish. He would dress more than 400 dozen of these flies a year.

In the late 1950s Royce fished the Wolf, and it worked its magic on him. Soon he was fishing it faithfully. He came to know the late Ed Haaga, and before long, Ed and Royce were exchanging ideas on tying techniques and patterns. If he arrived at Ed's home and found that Ed was out fishing, Royce would hang his new patterns on Ed's screen door next to the real insects that were there.

Although Ed had a strong influence on Royce's development as a tier, Royce's work is individual and creative, reflecting his own thoughts on pattern development. Much of this development is the result of fishing experience, but there is also evidence of the work of tiers such as Atherton, Wulff, Rosborough, and others.

Although he can and does tie dry flies of all styles, Royce favors heavily dressed patterns for his own fishing, a reflection of the hours he's spent fishing the broken water of the Wolf. And with those massive hands of his, he dresses his lovely drys in sizes as small as 22 with apparent ease.

One of Royce's unique patterns is a very effective caribou-hair mouse that he developed in the late 1960s for night fishing. One evening, he took seven trophy browns with this mammalian imitation. Although Royce gives his mouse ears and whiskers, it is not a pattern designed to charm people. Rather, it is a carefully thought-out design that creates the impression of a swimming rodent. When Royce's artificial mouse is retrieved with a pumping action, its skirt of goat and caribou hair pulses like the legs of a mouse frantically paddling for its life.

True, this big fly is strikingly effective for night-feeding browns foraging in the shallows under the alders, cedars, and hemlocks that hug the banks of the Wolf, but don't think that only Wolf River trout have fallen victim to this meaty morsel. It has taken big trout in spring creeks, New Zealand lakes, and Alaskan rivers, a tribute to Royce's creative fly designing.

The skills of this master fly tier have been shaped not only by the currents of the Wolf, but also by the currents of time, and if you think that Royce is a local tier, specializing in flies for Wisconsin's Wolf River, let me say that you're still standing in the shallows while Royce is way out there in deep water. His skills go vastly beyond his beginnings. Royce is a world-class fly tier and designer. His knowledge runs as deep and as broad as his beloved Wolf. And in the end, his skill has become artistry.

His techniques will make you pause and ponder. They'll drive you to the tying bench and test your mettle, investing you with new skills and polishing old ones. And you'll come away smiling and dreaming of soft spring days or early summer mornings when you'll baptize the new fly you've just created with one of Royce's tricks. I know; I've done just that.

—Gary Borger

PREFACE

I grew up on a fifteen-acre fruit farm in Kenosha, Wisconsin, in the south-eastern part of the state. In those days, Wisconsin farmers were completely self-sufficient. They depended on the family unit for sustenance and shelter.

My older brother Wilfred, my twin brother, Ralph, and I worked at neighboring farms weeding and picking vegetables during the summer months. I remember working on my hands and knees ten hours a day for ten cents an hour. Summer would pass, and winter would demand no less of us.

Two inches of frost on the inside walls of our farmhouse reminded us that winter would take its time yielding to spring. Mom would heat bricks in an old wood-burning cookstove. She wrapped them in towels, placing them at the foot of the bed my brothers and I slept in. Drifting off to sleep, with the cozy comfort of the warm bricks at my feet, my mind returned to the pleasant days of spring and summer. My father and I would each carry a fourteen-foot cane pole and a bucket of cornmeal balls in pursuit of carp for the family dinner. My dreams were not filled with visions of catching a trout on a fly. I knew nothing about the gentle sport of fly fishing that would one day consume my life.

The bricks cooled and deep slumber held my eyelids closed through the winter night. In the early morning, the banging of wood being tossed into the stove would drive the sleep away. The shocking cold would remind me of the work that had to be done. Life was good, but it was also hard.

Some of the great minds of psychology insist the events of our childhood impact our lives later on in ways we would never expect. Perhaps this is true. In 1933, when I was eight years old, my ten-year-old brother Wilfred was experimenting with blowing up cans. He had taken a tomato can and put gas into it. He ignited the fuel. The resulting "whoosh" caused him to panic. With a mounting fear of burning the garage down, he decided to toss the inferno outside. I had sneaked up to the garage to see what Wilfred was doing, and when he blindly threw his homemade firebomb it hit me.

In the early thirties, medical science was not what it is today. Burn injuries were usually crippling or fatal. Our local country doctor performed one of the country's first skin grafts on our kitchen table. He removed skin from my thigh and transferred it to my legs. Thanks to old Doc Lowe and my mother, who assisted with the surgery, my legs were saved, though badly scarred.

At the age of fourteen, another incident occurred that would affect my future. I was up in one of the snow-apple trees in our orchard, pruning withered branches, when a shot rang out. A bullet ripped through the leaves close to my body. One of my friends was messing around with a .22 rifle. He decided it would be funny to give me a start. I yelled out, "I don't think that's a bit funny." He answered with another shot that slammed into the trunk of the tree next to my head. I had all I was going to tolerate and scrambled down the ladder to fetch my own gun from the house. As I ran toward the house, another shot exploded behind me, ricocheting off a rock and embedding itself in my right calf.

The doctor decided I needed a tetanus shot. Within a few minutes my body began to react to the horse-serum antitoxin. My skin became covered with hives. Then my heart and breathing stopped. Adrenaline was pumped into my heart to get it beating again. My mother and father waited fearfully as the effects of the reaction that nearly killed me began to slip away. Once again, I recovered from a serious accident.

World War II shook our country like a nationwide earthquake. Patriotism was high and every able-bodied young man was eager to enlist in the armed services to do his part for our country. I was no exception. I wanted to be a Marine. I made several attempts to enlist. My medical history, severe scarring, and an inability to take tetanus shots were barriers to my enlistment. Persistence does pay, though. Finally, in 1943 I enlisted in the Marines. In two weeks I was off to boot camp. My first assignment out of boot camp was to guard an ammo-storage facility in San Francisco. In 1945 I was one of the soldiers in the campaign on Iwo Jima. The first Marines to set foot in Japan were thirty-four survivors of the original 210 soldiers in my company, of which I was one. We arrived in Japan on September 3, 1945. This historic moment marked the beginning of Japan's occupation by the Allied forces.

After my discharge, I started fishing to find peace from the experiences of World War II. My life seemed anticlimactic after the intense stresses of war. I needed a challenge for my mind, something to lay some of the more unpleasant memories to rest. I'm not sure how it all began. Somewhere along the way I was exposed to this concept, this challenge of fly fishing. The mystery associated with the sport intrigued me. Fly fishing became my postwar therapy.

I was like most people starting out in a new hobby. I did not know enough about it even to ask directions. I bought some cheap flies and tossed them around in lakes and ponds, catching panfish and bass. It really went against my upbringing to spend good money on flies that fell apart after catching only one or two fish. The store-bought flies I held in my hand looked easy enough to make. I decided to try making my own. I did not have much to lose. Who knows, I thought, maybe mine would last longer. My fly-tying career was under way.

I did not have a mentor to teach me fly tying, so I turned to books. I remember my first two fly-tying books. One was written by Joe Blades, the other by the renowned Helen Shaw. As I progressed as a tier, I invented better ways to do things. I started to develop some of my own techniques and patterns.

It was inevitable that I would be drawn into the esoteric world of fly fishing for trout. I became acquainted with Irwin Mann sometime in the 1950s. Irwin was a purist trout angler. His dedication to the pursuit of slick-skinned flashes of silver and gold seeped into my pores. I became a trout angler. I dedicated my efforts to developing flies to catch trout. Trout fishing is and will remain my first love in angling.

Wisconsin winters breed an illness known as "cabin fever." Anyone who has spent long, cold winters indoors looks for a diversion to maintain his sanity until spring releases him from this cruel confinement. My cure was the

Milwaukee Sports Show. Getting out and meeting new people with an interest in fly fishing was like a religious uplifting from the apathy of winter's deep freeze.

During one of my visits to the show, I was approached by Gary Borger. Gary is one of the finest fly fishers of our time. He asked if I would be interested in working as an instructor with his fly-fishing schools. I am sure that my casual response masked the thrill in my heart as I answered, "Does a bear live in the woods? I'm not jumping up and down in excitement. I just have a cramp in my foot." I worked as an instructor with Gary for eighteen years. I will always remember the opportunity he gave me.

In 1983, Gary Borger submitted my name to the Federation of Fly Fishers (FFF), recommending an invitation to tie at the International Conclave in West Yellowstone, Montana. When I received the invitation, I was excited and as nervous as a long-tailed cat in a room full of rocking chairs. I knew I would be tying with the best tiers in the country. The experience was more than I expected. I met people I had only read about. I learned from masters. Some have passed on. I was blessed with the stories and time they shared. Others are friends today, and will be always.

—Royce Dam

ACKNOWLEDGMENTS

Although they are too numerous to list, I would like to thank my friends and fellow fly tiers who encouraged me to write this book.

I owe a huge debt of gratitude to Mark Van Patten. I was concerned that I would not be able to translate my fly-tying techniques into print so that the reader would understand. Mark agreed to assist me in editing and rewriting. Without his help this book could never have been done.

I want to thank Thom J. Beck for his superb photography. Thom is not a fly tier, yet he was able to produce what I believe are some of the best photographs that I have ever seen.

My good friend Peter McCauley assisted me with his computer skills, turning my handwritten work into printed pages.

Special thanks must go to my longtime friend Gary Borger for his Foreword. Gary has been a great supporter for years. He was responsible for my invitation to my first FFF International Conclave.

I also would like to thank Carla Widener, who for many years has encouraged and supported me in all my fly-tying endeavors.

In addition, I would like to thank the following sponsors:

Danville Chenille Co., Inc.
1 Hampstead Road
P.O. Box 1000
Danville, NH 03819-1000
(603) 382-5553

Dan Bailey's Fly Shop
209 West Park Street
P.O. Box 1019
Livingston, MT 59047-1019
(800) 356-4052

Blue Mountain Angler
1375 Barleen Drive
Walla Walla, WA 99362
(509) 539-8733

Uni Products, Inc.
561 Rue Princpale
Ste. Melanic, Quebec JOK 3AO

Wapsi Fly, Inc.
27CR 485
Mountain Home, AR 72653
(870) 425-9500

Fly Rite, Inc.
Dept F.F.
7421 S. Beyer
Frankenmouth, MI 48734
(517) 652-9869

Dyna King
Abby Precision Mfg. Co.
70 Industrial Drive
Cloverdale, CA 95425
(707) 894-5566

Angler Sport Group, Inc.
6619 Oak Orchard Road
Elba, NY 14058
(716) 757-9959

Joe Humphreys
1051 Boalsburg Road
Boalsburg, PA 16827
(814) 466-6085

Gordon Griffiths
1190 Genella
Waterford, MI 48328
(810) 673-7701

CHAPTER 1

Tools

Advances in fly-tying tools and materials make those I started tying with look like antiques. Fly-tying techniques, however, have not evolved to keep pace with changes in tools and materials. One of the purposes of this book is to share some new and efficient approaches to fly tying, a system that will let you capitalize on time-saving advances. First, though, we should look at the tools you will need.

VISES

Your vise is the single most expensive tool you will buy, and the most important. Buy the best one you can afford. Vises vary a lot in design and features, but we can make a few general comments about what you get for your money.

A lower-priced vise usually has a stationary head. The head and jaws are fixed at a 30-degree angle above horizontal. You cannot adjust the angle of the head to make the vise more comfortable to use or to accommodate a particular hook. Nor can you rotate the head while tying to view every side of a fly. Usually, the jaws

are made of softer metal that will wear more quickly than the material used in more costly vises. This will make their hook-holding ability considerably shorter lived.

Medium-priced vises generally have heads that can be adjusted up or down. Some have rotating heads, which allow you to turn a fly to look at all sides without

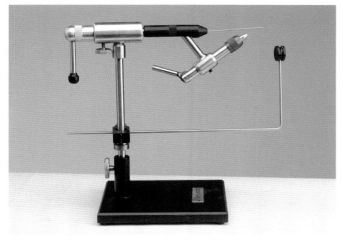

A Dyna-King Barracuda vise. This is a true rotary vise with a centering gauge to center the hook shank. A quality tool such as this will hold any hook you need it to hold and will last a lifetime.

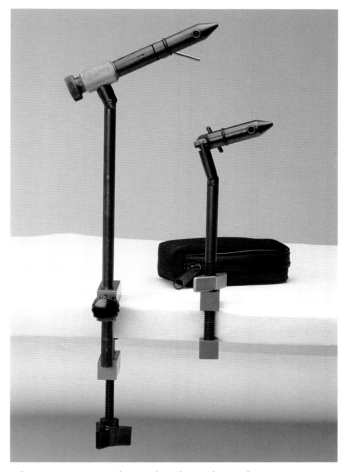

Blue Mountain Anglers makes the mid-priced rotating vise on the left. The angle of the head can be adjusted, and the entire head can rotate to let you examine every side of a fly. On the right is a Blue Mountain Anglers travel vise. This vise is ideal to take on trips for on-stream tying.

removing it from the vise. The metal of which the jaws are made is usually higher in quality, and the jaws will last for a long time.

Higher-priced, professional-grade vises are true rotary designs. They are usually guaranteed for many years; some have lifetime guarantees. Vises in the higher price range often have interchangeable jaws to hold hooks of all sizes efficiently. These vises hold hooks from size 8/0 all the way down to size 26, and will hold any hook securely.

The most important feature of any vise is the jaws. Make sure the jaws hold a hook tightly. Try the different hook sizes that you will most likely use in your fly tying. Remember, the vise is your main tool for tying, so choose wisely within your budget.

SCISSORS

Scissors are another important tool in fly tying. Two important characteristics are sharp points for detail trimming and a serrated edge on one blade. It is also important that you find scissors with finger loops large enough to fit your fingers.

BOBBINS

A bobbin with a ceramic tube works best. I usually have a couple within easy reach, one designed for use with fine thread and another for heavier thread. Another bobbin to consider is one with a flared end; this style is used when working with floss.

BODKINS

This versatile tool is nothing more than a needle with a handle. A bodkin is used for picking out dubbing, cleaning out hook eyes, applying head cement, and many other tasks. I like one that has a hexagonal handle, which keeps the tool from rolling around on the table and disappearing when you need it.

HACKLE PLIERS

There are many types of hackle pliers: teardrop, English style, and rotary, to name a few. Some hackle pliers have a pad on one side of the jaws, others have pads on both sides. Most have no pads. The choice is up to you. In my experience, one type is as good as another.

OTHER TOOLS

You don't need a great many tools to tie flies, but many of us buy more and different tools just because we want them. Usually, these find their way into a corner somewhere and are never used again. It is a common malady known as "gadget addiction." However, there are some gadgets that are nice to have. The following fall into this category.

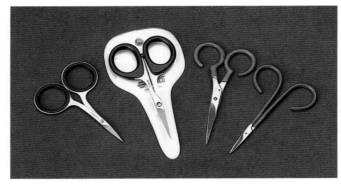

Good fly-tying scissors have sharp points for detail work and a finely serrated edge on one blade. Make sure the finger loops are large enough for your hands.

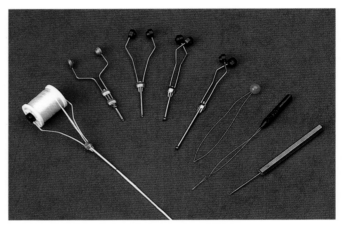

It pays to have several good bobbins: one for fine thread, one for heavier thread, and one for floss. A bobbin threader (second and third items from far right) makes it easier to load a bobbin. A bodkin (far right) has many uses in fly tying.

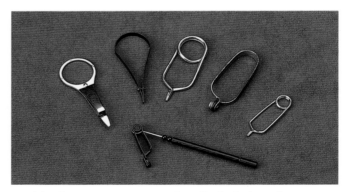

Hackle pliers come in many styles, all of which work. It's handy to have more than one of these tools.

• A pair of pliers with smooth jaws. These are used to flatten the stems of feathers that will roll when being tied in place.

• A bobbin threader, which makes it easier to get the thread through the tube of a bobbin.

• A dubbing teaser, for picking out fibers on a fly's body.

• A whip finisher and half-hitch tools, for securing the thread when you finish a fly.

• A dubbing-loop tool, for twisting fur, wool, or some other material inside a loop of thread.

• A vise extension, which moves your work closer to you and puts it at a more comfortable height. Reaching to tie your flies will make your arms, neck, and back muscles sore after long periods of tying.

• A good tying lamp. A fluorescent light is a good choice. You may prefer a different kind of lighting, so choose the one you like best.

• A profile plate. Working against a light-colored background makes it easier to see what you are doing. Profile plates attach to your vise or table and provide a light background behind your tying area. A piece of light-colored plastic or cardboard propped against a cup of coffee works pretty well, too.

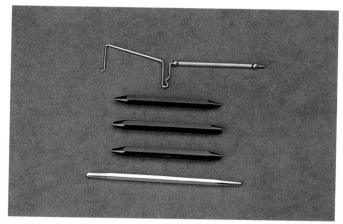

A whip-finisher (top) or a half-hitch tool (four examples are shown) is used to make a knot that secures the thread when you finish a fly. Although you can make a whip-finish knot or half hitch by hand, many tiers find it easier to use a tool.

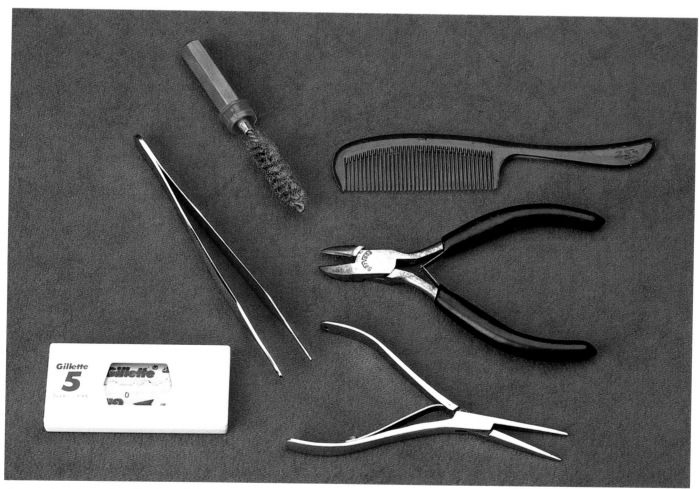

Among the other tools a fly tier will find useful are (clockwise from bottom left) razor blades, extra-fine tweezers, a dubbing teaser, a fine-toothed comb, small cutting pliers, and small, smooth-jawed pliers.

CHAPTER 2

Tying Wet Flies

Before we start tying our first fly, there are a few things you need to know. Clamping a hook in your vise, attaching the thread to the hook, and securing the thread to finish a fly are skills you will use on every pattern. Some of the flies we're going to tie have bodies made of dubbing. Since both the dubbing material (wool) and the method I use might be unfamiliar to you, we'll take a quick look at the basics of my dubbing technique.

CLAMPING THE HOOK

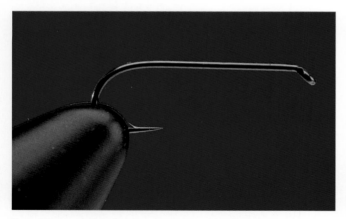

Put the hook in the vise's jaws with the shank horizontal. Be sure to put enough of the bend of the hook in the jaws. Do not try to clamp only a small portion of the bend. I like to have the barb of the hook exposed, with most of the bend clamped in the vise.

ATTACHING THE THREAD

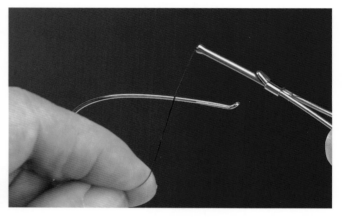

1. Hold the bobbin in your right hand. Grasp the end of the thread with your left thumb and index finger. Pull several inches of thread from the bobbin. Hold the thread over the top of the hook shank, with the bobbin on the far side and the tag end of the thread on the near side. Keep the thread taut.

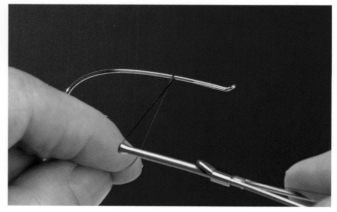

2. Make a wrap around the hook shank by bringing the bobbin down, beneath the hook, and toward you. This is the standard direction for wrapping tying thread: away from you over the hook, and toward you beneath the hook. Viewed from the front of the hook, the thread travels in a clockwise direction.

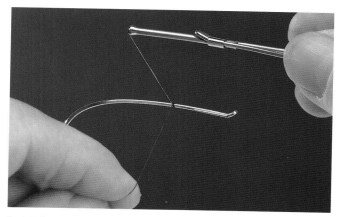

3. Make another wrap, overlapping the thread on top of the shank. You're wrapping the working thread over the tag end, jamming the thread against the hook shank. If you keep tension on the thread at all times, you should have no problem wrapping it and getting it to hold against the shank.

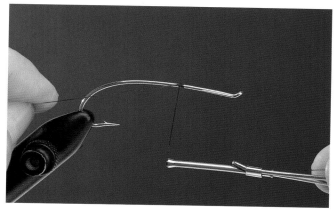

4. After making several wraps of thread, hold the tag end at a 30-degree angle on the near side of the hook shank. By keeping the tag end tight and at an angle to the hook, you can use it to guide subsequent wraps into po-sition on the hook. Keep the wraps close together as you work.

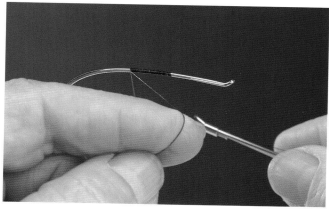

5. When you have covered as much of the hook shank as you want, break off the tag end of the thread. To do this, hold the bobbin on the far side of the hook and keep the thread tight. With your left hand, make a quick jerk of the tag end toward the hook eye. The tag end will break at the wraps on the hook shank.

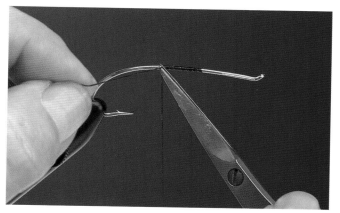

6. Another way to remove the tag end is simply to snip it with your scissors. Breaking it off saves a little time, since you don't have to pick up your scissors. With heavy thread, however, cutting the tag end is often easier.

MAKING DUBBING WITH WOOL

You can make the bodies of flies with many different materials, but you will apply nearly any material with one of two methods. The most obvious method is to tie a piece of material to the hook and then wrap the stuff around the shank. This is how you cover a hook with chenille, yarn, floss, tinsel, and other materials.

The other method is called dubbing, and it consists of twisting fur, wool, or some other material onto the tying thread, and then wrapping the dubbed thread around the hook shank. This is among the oldest and most important fly-tying techniques.

Many of the flies described in this book have bodies dubbed with wool. To make wool dubbing, you'll need a pair of wire brushes used to brush long hair on animals. These brushes can be purchased at a pet shop. Look for brushes that have stainless-steel wires.

The other component is, of course, wool, which you can purchase on the hide, tanned. Fly shops and catalog houses sell patches of wool in many colors. I use wool for dubbing almost all my dry flies, wets, and nymphs. I've been asked many times, "Won't wool dubbing sink your dry fly?" My reply is, "Yes, but I use a dry-fly floatant on my dry flies." If your dry flies do not have a coating of something to protect them, they would absorb water and sink. I have worked with just about every kind of fur, and they will all sink without some kind of floatant. I like wool because it is very easy to work with.

When buying a patch of wool, look for hair that is around two inches in length. Feel the hair. The best wool feels very soft and has a fine texture.

Dubbing also comes from many kinds of animals, and is made from a variety of synthetic fibers. The fur of muskrats, beavers, rabbits, raccoons, and foxes are just a few of the natural dubbing materials. Antron is probably the best known synthetic fiber used for dubbing, but many other synthetics have been put to use by fly tiers. I prefer wool dubbing because it is easy to work with and because it goes a long way. Wool can be purchased in all the colors used for tying flies, and colors can be mixed together to create new shades. You can even combine synthetic material with wool to produce dubbing that has some sparkle; I'll show you how in a little while. First, you need to learn how to prepare wool.

1. Essentially, you're going to use a pair of wire brushes to card the wool.

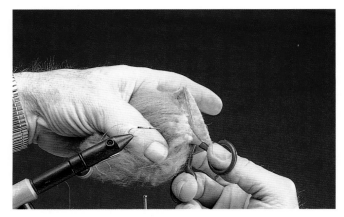

2. Cut the wool as close to the hide as possible. Do not cut the wool into pieces; you want the fibers left long.

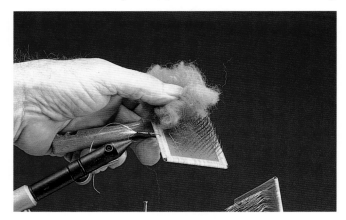

3. Place a small amount of wool on one of the brushes. Place the other brush on top, forming a wool sandwich. Press the brushes together, then pull them in opposite directions, allowing the wires to pull the wool fibers apart.

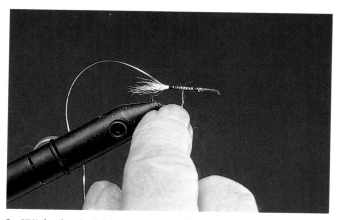

4. Keep repeating the brushing operation until all the wool fibers are separated and carded into a neat clump. That's all there is to it; the material is now ready to be used.

USING CARDED WOOL FOR DUBBING

After carding the wool, you will notice the uneven fibers extending beyond the edge of the brush. When you remove material from the brush, grab only the tips of the wool. As you pull these longer fibers from the brush, others will follow.

How much wool to use depends on the size of the fly you are tying. With a little practice, you will learn to select the right amount for any hook.

1. Pull a little wool from the brush. You don't need much—grab only the tips of the fibers, and draw out a small clump of material.

2. With the bobbin in your left hand, angle the thread away from the hook shank. Keep the thread tight. Tack the fibers between your right index finger and thumb to the thread. Press your index finger and thumb together and twist the wool onto the thread. Twist in one direction only—do not go back and forth. From above, the direction is always counterclockwise.

3. With the tips of the wool attached to the thread, move your finger and thumb farther down, grasping the wool along with the tying thread, and cradle the bobbin in the butt of your hand. Start to wrap the wool around the hook shank. As you wind the dubbing, keep the opening between your index finger and thumb toward the hook shank. This helps to avoid rubbing your fingertips against the dubbing and pulling it from the thread.

After making several wraps, you will notice that the wool is starting to twist itself around the thread. To twist the dubbing more tightly and produce a tighter, slimmer body, hold the thread and dubbing closer to the hook shank when making your wraps. For a looser, fuzzier body, hold the thread and dubbing farther from the hook as you wrap. Generally, the smaller the hook, the closer to it you hold your index finger and thumb; with a larger hook, hold the thread and dubbing farther from the shank.

After practicing this dubbing technique, you will be surprised how much time you can save tying flies this way, compared to the conventional method of twisting all the dubbing tightly around the thread before you start wrapping it around the hook. This technique works particularly well with wool, which is one of the reasons I like this material. We'll look at this method in greater detail later in the book, when we start tying flies with dubbed bodies.

ADDING SPARKLE TO DUBBING

Antron yarn (rug yarn) can be purchased in many colors useful to fly tiers. It is often called sparkle yarn. Adding this synthetic material creates dubbing that catches and reflects light.

To add sparkle to your dubbing, cut the Antron yarn into pieces, about an inch to an inch and a quarter in length. Add the pieces of yarn to one of your carding brushes, and work the brushes against each other to separate the fibers, just as you do with wool. Card the Antron yarn by itself, and then add it to wool to get the amount of sparkle you would like your dubbing to have.

THE HALF HITCH

This knot secures the thread when you have finished a fly. After making two or three half hitches at the head of a fly, you can clip the thread, apply a drop of head cement to the fly, and begin another. The fly in the photos is a rather complex mouse pattern, but the procedure is the same on any fly.

1. Hold the bobbin on the near side of the hook shank with your left hand. Pull about ten inches of thread from the bobbin. Hold the bobbin toward you with the thread at about a 45-degree angle from the hook shank.

2. Place your right index and second finger on top of the thread in the shape of a V.

3. Raise the bobbin above the hook.

4. Turn your index finger and second finger over so that they point up, with the pads of your fingers facing you. As you turn your fingers over, move the bobbin rearward and to the near side of the hook, and bring your index finger to the front of the hook eye. You want the thread to cross over itself, as shown.

5. Place the thread that is around your index finger behind the hook eye. Lower your index finger to guide the thread under the hook and to the far side of the eye. Then raise your finger until your hand is in the position shown.

6. Slip your second finger out of the loop of thread. Keep your index finger in the loop, and be careful to keep tension on the thread at all times.

7. Put your second finger on the far side of the fly's head to hold the thread in place. Pinch the loop with your index finger and thumb, and move them to the front of the hook eye. You can now guide the loop to the head of the fly with your index finger and thumb while pulling the bobbin rearward to tighten the knot. This will complete the half hitch. Make two or three half hitches before cutting the thread and adding cement.

If you're a beginner, practice attaching the thread, wrapping it around the hook, and making half hitches. Thread control is the first and most important skill to learn, and it will enable you to make neat, sturdy flies.

THE GRIZZLY HACKLE

Our first fly will teach you several things: making and attaching a tail, winding a body, and wrapping a wet-fly hackle. In the materials list, I first specify the materials shown in the photos, and then, in parentheses, optional or substitute materials. This gives you some leeway in selecting materials. Most of the materials lists in this book follow this pattern.

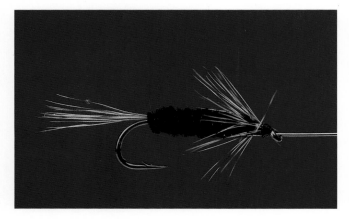

The Grizzly Hackle

Hook:	Size 8, 1X-long wet-fly hook, such as a Daiichi 1560, Tiemco 3761, Dai Riki 060, or Mustad 3906B.
Thread:	Black prewaxed 12/0 (or prewaxed black 6/0 or 8/0).
Tail:	Fibers from a grizzly hen hackle (or from a grizzly saddle hackle or schlappen feather).
Body:	Fine black chenille (or wool dubbing).
Hackle:	Grizzly hen hackle (or a grizzly saddle hackle).

1. Select a wet-fly hackle, one that has mostly webby fibers.

2. Strip the fluff from the butt end of the feather.

3. Hold the feather by its tip and select the amount of material needed for the tail.

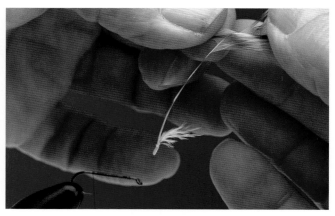

4. Grasp the fibers tightly and pull them from the hackle stem.

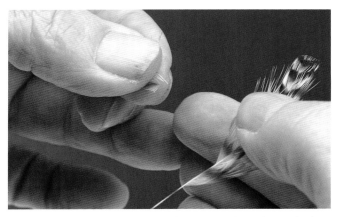

5. The fibers should come off in a neat bunch, with their butt ends fairly even.

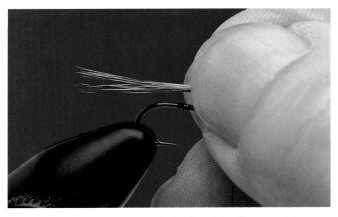

6. Grasp the butt ends of the hackle fibers with your right index finger and thumb. Hold the fibers over the top of the hook shank, near the bend of the hook.

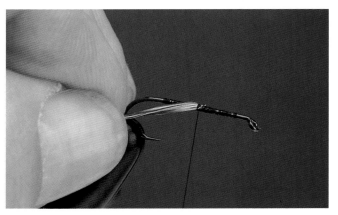

7. Grab the fibers with your left thumb and forefinger. Bring the thread over the top of the hook and down on the far side. Tighten the thread by pulling the bobbin downward. As you tighten the thread, pinch the fibers against the hook shank and press your index finger against the hook. This keeps the tail from rolling to the far side of the hook. With the thread tight, relax your index finger and thumb and move them closer to the tips of the fibers. Hold the tail fibers at a slight angle to you and continue your wraps toward the bend of the hook.

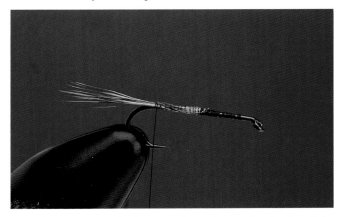

8. When you reach the spot just above the barb of the hook, start wrapping forward, toward the butts of the tail fibers.

9. Wrap forward to a spot just in front of the middle of the shank. The tail fibers should be on top of the hook, like these, with their butts neatly bound down.

10. The body is made of fine (or "small" chenille). Cut a piece several inches long.

11. Use your thumbnail to strip the fuzz from the end of the chenille. This will reveal the core of the chenille, which consists of two strings.

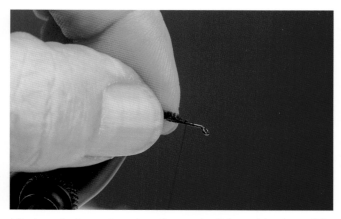

12. Attach the strings just forward of the midpoint of the hook. Once the chenille is attached, advance the thread to within one hook-eye length of the front of the shank.

13. Wrap the chenille back to the rear of the hook, stopping at the end of the thread wraps securing the tail.

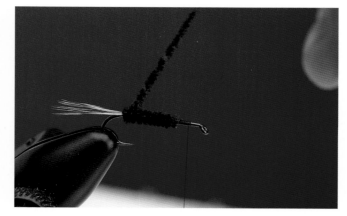

14. Overlap the last wrap of chenille. Then wind the chenille forward, using side-by-side wraps.

15. Stop where the thread is hanging, one hook-eye length from the front of the shank. Tie off the chenille against the bottom of the hook shank.

16. With the tips of your scissors, cut away the leftover chenille. Be careful not to cut the thread.

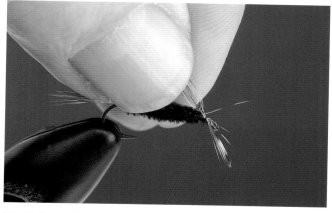

17. Select a hackle feather that has a great deal of web. Strip the fluff from the butt end. Separate the fibers at the tie-in point of the stem. Position the hackle at the front of the body. Make your first couple of thread wraps around the hackle stem.

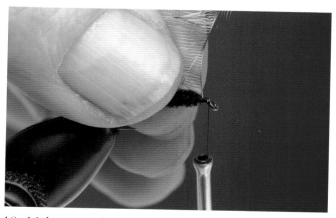

18. Make your third wrap in front of the hackle stem. Make another wrap behind the stem, returning the thread to the original tie-in spot. Fold the tip of the hackle to the rear and make a few wraps over it. This locks in the feather so that it cannot pull out. Now cut away the excess hackle tip. Make a wrap to bring the thread to the back of the hook eye.

19. Start winding the hackle. Pull the fibers to the rear as you make each wrap. Wind the feather forward, making each wrap in front of the last.

20. Stop when you reach the eye of the hook. Note how the hackle wrapped around the hook slopes to the rear.

21. Make a wrap of thread to catch the hackle stem, and then fold the stem to the rear. Start wrapping toward the rear of the fly's head, binding the stem to the hook as you go. Once again, you are locking the feather to the hook.

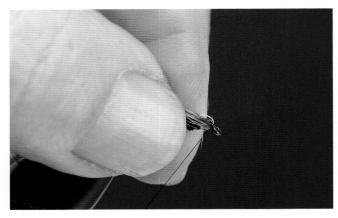

22. Pull the hackle fibers and the rest of the feather back, and bring your thread wraps to the rear of the fly's head. Cut away the remainder of the feather. Shape the head with several wraps of thread, and secure the thread with three half hitches.

23. Clip the thread, and your Grizzly Hackle wet fly is finished. Apply a drop of cement to the head.

THE PASS LAKE

Early one spring, my friend Carla and I headed for the Brule River in northern Wisconsin. We arrived at daybreak and were welcomed with a few threatening clouds in the sky. I love a little overcast for fishing. With a great spot in mind, Carla and I walked along the river's edge enjoying the scents and sights nature provided.

A light rain began to fall. What a beautiful spring morning for catching fish! Then all hell broke loose and the rain poured down as if someone had dumped a barrel of water on us. We quickly took shelter under a pine thicket, not wanting to get soaked before we cast a line.

Carla was the first to notice the rain had begun to ease up a little. "Let's fish our way back to the car in case it starts to pour again," she said. Not long after we began fishing I started to catch a chill and needed to get to the car for a change of clothes.

Dry clothing made me feel like fishing again, and we headed back upstream. Carla wanted to start where we had left the stream earlier. I took a position above Carla to fish the spaces between the alders. Carla has a little more trouble putting her fly in such tight spots.

I had on a size 8 Pass Lake wet fly. In just a couple of casts I had a strike. Understand, this was not just an ordinary sip-and-splash. It was more like a toilet flushing. The sound of a large fish taking my fly got Carla's attention. She reeled in her line and headed my way to watch the show.

I was standing waist deep in fast water and realized I could get in trouble. I got the fish on the reel and reached around for my net, only to realize that I had left it in the car when I changed my clothes. I knew I couldn't land this fish without a net, especially in this fast water. I asked Carla to run to the car and get my net.

While Carla was retrieving my net, I slowly worked the fish to improve my position on the bank. I would gain some line and the fish would rip it off my reel just as quickly.

I finally got in position to land the fish as Carla appeared through the alders with my net. As she handed me the net, the fish managed one last burst of energy and leaped into the air. I swear it flew right over my shoulder. A pull on the line snapped me back to reality and I knew the fish was still on. It measured over 20 inches and had that well-fed, chunky look of a wild Brule River trout.

I released the fish in the hope that another angler might have the same experience. Who knows? Maybe I'll meet up with that fish again someday. The Pass Lake had served me well once again.

It will serve you well, too, so let's tie one. The tail and body of the Pass Lake are made with the same tech-

niques used to tie the Grizzly Hackle, though the tie-in spot for the chenille is slightly different. On the Pass Lake, we'll make a wing with calf-body hair, and tie a beard-style hackle rather than a collar.

The Pass Lake

Hook:	1X-long wet-fly hook, size 6 to 16, such as a Daiichi 1560, Tiemco 3761, Dai Riki 060, or Mustad 3906B.
Thread:	Prewaxed black 12/0 (or black 6/0 or 8/0; size 3/0 on the largest flies).
Tail:	Brown hackle fibers.
Body:	Fine black chenille (extra fine on the smallest flies; medium on the largest).
Wing:	White calf-body hair (calf tail on larger flies).
Hackle:	Fibers from a brown hen-neck or back feather (or from a saddle hackle or schlappen feather).

1. Make the tail as you did on the Grizzly Hackle wet fly. After tying in the tail, wind the thread to a spot about one and a half hook-eye lengths in front of the center of the shank. Tying in the chenille here will give the body a forward taper that lets the wing sit lower on the body. If you would like the wing to ride higher, just move the tie-in spot for the chenille forward a little. After attaching the chenille, wrap the body as you did on the Grizzly Hackle.

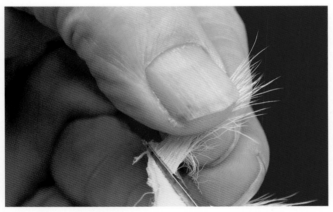

2. Grasp the amount of hair needed for the wing with your left index finger and thumb. I position the second finger of my right hand underneath the patch of hide when selecting and cutting the hair; this gives me something to push against with my left index finger and thumb. Press the hide against the second finger of your right hand and trap the hairs between your left index finger and thumb. Pull the hairs away from the hide just enough to allow you to insert the scissors blade underneath the clump.

3. After cutting the hair, remove the fuzz and short fibers from the butt ends. Simply hold the clump about halfway between tips and butts, and, with your right hand, pull the short fibers and fuzz from the bottom of the clump.

4. Grasp the butt ends with your right index finger and thumb. Pick out the longest, most uneven hairs at the tip end, even if you reduce the amount of hair. You probably have more than you need anyway. With the butt ends between your right index finger and thumb, hold the hair atop the hook with your thumb at the front of the hook. Measure the length needed for the wing; it should extend from the front of the hook eye to the bend of the hook.

5. Once you have the correct length, grasp the hair at the rear of the hook eye with your left index finger and thumb. Your thumbnail now marks the tie-in spot.

6. Cut the hair at the front of your thumbnail. If you wait to cut the hair until after tying it to the hook, you will probably disturb the alignment or shape of the wing. That's why we cut off the excess hair now.

7. Position the hair on top of the hook shank and line up the butt ends with the back of the hook eye. With the hair in position, add a small drop of head cement underneath the hair. This will help to prevent the hair from spreading, and will also ensure that the cement reaches the bottom hairs of the wing. Make one turn of thread over and around the hair and hook shank, and add just a little pressure to hold the hair in place. Then make a second wrap of thread around the hair, this time adding pressure straight downward to secure the hair.

8. Tie the hair in place, making several tight, smooth wraps toward the hook eye.

9. Select a feather to be used for the beard hackle. Strip off the fibers needed for the beard. Position the fibers underneath the hook shank, using your right index finger and thumb. The fibers should just about reach the point of the hook.

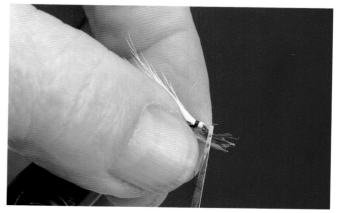

10. Once you have the correct length, grasp the fibers with your left index finger and thumb. Now cut the fibers even with the hook eye. Don't cut the butts too short; if you cut them farther back, the chance of losing the fibers increases.

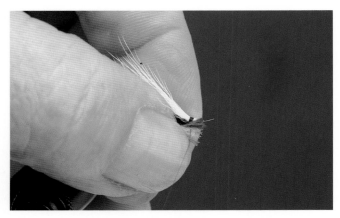

11. Tie the fibers to the underside of the hook, directly below where you attached the wing.

12. With the beard in place, half-hitch the thread two or three times, cut it, and cement the head.

THE ROYAL COACHMAN WET

The Royal Coachman has been around a long time, and it's still hanging in there. It's a good attractor pattern, but that's not the main reason I've included it here. I want to introduce you to techniques for applying peacock herl and for making the quill-slip wings used on many traditional wet flies.

The Royal Coachman Wet

Hook:	1X-long wet-fly hook such as a Daiichi 1560, Tiemco 3761, Dai Riki 060, or Mustad 3906B, size 8 to 16.
Thread:	Black 10/0.
Tail:	Golden pheasant tippets or brown hackle fibers, as shown.
Body:	A butt of peacock herl, then red floss, then more peacock herl.
Hackle:	Coachman-brown saddle or hen hackle.
Wings:	White goose-quill slips.

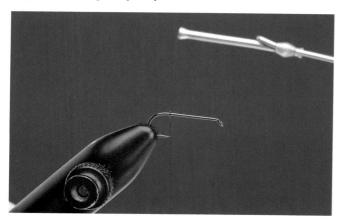

1. Attach the thread to the hook just above the point. Wrap back to the spot halfway between the point of the hook and the barb. Cut the tag end or break it off.

2. Select a hackle feather. Separate the number of fibers you will need for the fly's tail. Strip the fibers from the feather.

3. With your left thumb and forefinger, hold the clump of fibers in postion at the rear of the hook. Bring the thread up between your thumb and the butts of the tail, and down on the far side of the hook between the butts of the tail and the tip of your index finger.

4. Tighten the thread by pulling the bobbin downward. After tightening the first wrap of thread, make several more. Wind forward and then back, but stop before you reach the rearmost wrap of thread securing the tail. You want to have a little space between the thread and that rearmost wrap.

5. Select a strand of herl from an eyed peacock feather. I prefer the material close to the eye of the feather, because the herl there has finer fibers.

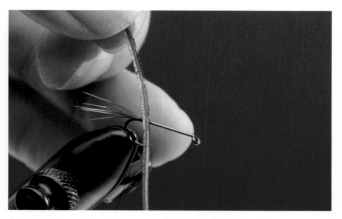

6. Note that the fibers on the strand of herl slant toward one side of the quill. Tie the herl to the hook so that the fibers face down. This will give the rear of the butt section a rounded shape. Tie on the herl with several wraps of thread, stopping at the spot just above the hook point.

7. Notice the space between the tie-in wraps for the herl and the rearmost wrap securing the tail fibers. This space helps to prevent breaking the herl when you start to wrap it. If you were to tie in the herl at the rearmost wrap of the tail, you would have a much greater likelihood of cutting the quill with the thread.

8. Start wrapping the herl, using clockwise turns as viewed from the front of the hook. Angle the first wrap back toward the base of the tail. Make one wrap at the base of the tail, then cross over toward the front and continue wrapping to the spot directly above the point of the hook.

9. Tie off the herl with two wraps of thread. Break off the tag end. Wind the thread forward to the spot shown, about two hook-eye lengths behind the front of the shank.

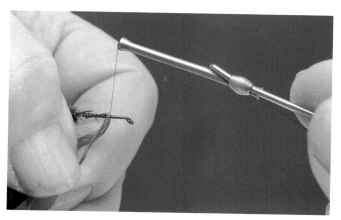

10. Loop a piece of floss around the thread, with the short end of the material on the far side of the thread. Hold both ends of the floss together with your left index finger and thumb. Make a wrap of thread around the hook shank, and tighten the wrap to draw the floss to the hook. Then make one complete wrap of thread around the shank in front of the doubled-over floss.

11. Release the short end of the floss and continue making thread wraps to the rear. The first half-dozen wraps should be snug, but not too tight.

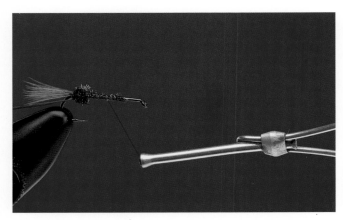

12. After making a few thread wraps to the rear, pull on the long end of the floss to draw the short end underneath the thread wraps. Continue your thread wraps, stopping short of the peacock-herl butt. Then wrap the thread forward to within one hook-eye length of the front of the shank.

13. Make the first wrap of floss right in front of the peacock-herl butt. Continue to wrap the floss forward until you reach the spot where the thread is hanging.

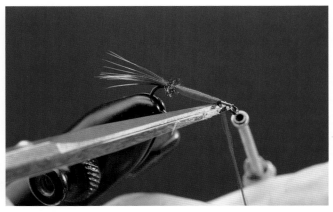

14. Tie off the floss with a few snug turns of thread. Hold the thread at an angle on the far side of the hook, and, with the tips of your scissors, clip the excess floss.

15. Tie in several strands of herl at the front of the floss. Wrap the strands of herl around the thread three or four times. Grasp the herl and thread near the end of the strands. Wrap the herl and thread first to the rear, stopping just short of the center of the hook, and then to the front, stopping at the original tie-in point. Secure the herl with two wraps of thread and cut away the excess.

16. Select a feather for the hackle. The fibers should be long enough to reach slightly past the hook point.

17. Stroke the fibers toward the butt of the feather, and tie in the feather by its tip with a couple of wraps of thread.

18. Fold the hackle tip to the rear and tie it down with another couple of thread wraps. Clip the excess tip. This method locks the feather to the hook so that it will not pull out.

19. Wrap the hackle collar, folding the fibers to the rear as you do. Don't make the hackle too heavy; two or three wraps will do.

20. Secure the hackle stem with a couple of wraps of thread. Then fold the stem to the rear and bind it down, locking the feather to the hook.

21. Clip the leftover hackle feather.

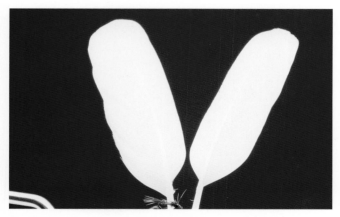

22. Select a matching pair of goose quills, one from the left wing and one from the right wing.

23. Cut a section from each wing quill. The width of each section should be about half the gap of the hook.

24. Place the two wing sections together with the good sides out. Align the tips of the two sections. Hold the wings at the top of the hook shank with your right index finger and thumb. The tips of the wings should reach the bend of the hook.

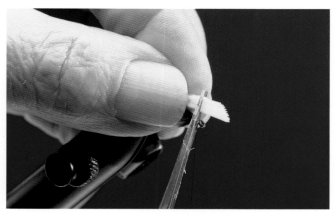

25. Grasp the wings with your left index finger and thumb. Hold them with the tips even and a little lower than the hook shank. Cut the wing butts even with the center of the fly's head. If you trim the butts later, after attaching the wing sections to the hook, you will probably knock the wings out of alignment. Trimming the butts now eliminates that problem.

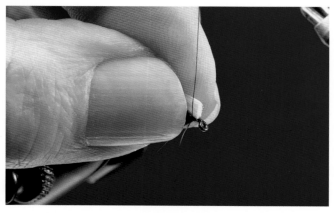

26. Before tying on the wings, put a small drop of head cement at the tie-in spot. This will help to hold the wings in place and keep them from sliding. With the wings in position, make one turn of thread around the butts.

27. With the bobbin beneath the fly, start to apply downward pressure with the thread. Use the tip of your index finger to keep the wings in place on top of the shank.

28. Keep the thread tight while you move your thumb and index finger a little to the rear. Then continue the tie-down wraps for the wings, building the fly's head in the process.

29. Tie off the thread and apply a drop of cement to finish your Royal Coachman wet fly.

THE HAIRWING ROYAL COACHMAN

Our next fly is a hairwing version of the Royal Coachman wet. Wings made of calf tail are more durable than the quill sections traditionally used on wet flies, and for that reason are preferred by some anglers. Except for the wing, this fly uses the same materials as the standard Royal Coachman. We will, however, take a more detailed look at using the tying thread to reinforce the peacock herl for the front section of the body, and we'll give our hairwing fly a beard hackle rather than a collar.

1. Construct the tail, peacock-herl butt, and floss section of the body as you did on the previous fly. Cut three pieces of herl from an eyed peacock feather, and tie them in by the tips at the front of the floss.

2. Wrap the pieces of herl around the tying thread. Make sure to wrap them in a counterclockwise direction, as viewed from above. Grab the herl and thread near the end of the pieces, and, without applying too much pressure, begin wrapping the material around the hook. Wrap to the rear first, covering the area needed for the front section of the body. Then reverse direction, wrapping to the front until you reach the original tie-in point. Secure the herl and cut the excess.

3. Separate a clump of calf-tail hair large enough to make the fly's wing. Hold the clump tightly, as shown, and cut the hair from the tail.

4. Pick out the fuzz and short hairs from the clump. Grab the butts of the hair with your right hand, and hold the clump over the hook to establish the length of the wing. The wing should reach from the hook eye to the bend of the hook.

5. After establishing the length of the wing, grasp the clump with your left hand, with your thumbnail even with the hook eye. Cut the hair at the front of your left thumbnail, giving you the length needed for the wing.

6. Put a small drop of cement at the tie-in spot for the hair. Hold the cut end of the clump at the center of the fly's head. Make a wrap of thread over the hair and to the bottom of the hook. Apply just enough pressure to hold the hair in position. Continue around the hair with a second wrap. When you reach the bottom of the hook, tighten the thread, pressing your left index finger and thumb together and pulling down with the bobbin. Continue to make tight wraps, binding down the butts of the hair.

7. From a brown hackle feather, strip clumps of fibers for the fly's beard. Hold the fibers beneath the hook. The tips of the beard should reach the point of the hook.

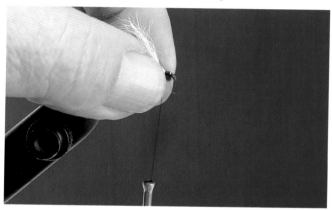

8. Transfer the hackle fibers to your left hand and cut the butts to length. Hold the fibers against the bottom of the fly and secure them with several wraps of thread.

9. Make a few more wraps of thread to shape the fly's head. Tie off the thread with a half hitch and apply cement to the head.

THE RED LLAMA

A friend and I were fishing the Wolf River in northern Wisconsin early one spring when a storm forced us to cover. We stood under a spread of pines and talked about the fishing we had been enjoying before the rain started. As it usually does with us, the talk turned to flies. It turned out that we had both been using the same pattern, a Red Llama wet fly. This pattern, we knew, was the creation of a man named Miles Turtlelot, and we also knew that he lived somewhere on an Indian reservation not too far from where we were fishing.

Neither my friend nor I knew exactly where Miles lived, but we decided that since the day was shot anyway, we would go and try to find him. We drove around for a while and asked a few directions. Finally, we pulled up to the Turtlelot home. After a few knocks, someone answered the door. Standing in the doorway was a small man. I asked if Miles was in and he replied, "I am Miles Turtlelot. Who are you?"

After a brief introduction, I decided to get down to business. I asked Miles if I could purchase a few of his famous Red Llamas. We were invited into his home and led to a small room. I think his fly-tying room was actually a closet. It seemed to fit Miles well enough. The table was strewn with assorted tying materials and a few finished flies, some of which were Red Llamas. Miles invited me to take what I wanted. I scooped up three Llamas and asked what I owed him. His firm price was only a buck. You don't forget experiences like that day. Meeting a master fly tier for the first time and being invited into his inner sanctuary is a rare event.

I noticed some of the other patterns lying on the desk, and discovered that Miles tied Pass Lake wets by the gross. On my next trip to Miles's house, I brought a gift of twenty-five choice white calf tails. It's not that I'm exceedingly generous—at the time, calf tails sold for a dime apiece. That gesture, however, was the first brick in the foundation of a lifelong friendship.

The Red Llama is tied both as a wet fly and as a streamer. Either style is an excellent fish catcher. Here's the wet-fly version.

2. Remove six to eight fibers from a grizzly hackle. The tail should be as long as the gap of the hook is wide. Attach the tail, making your wraps toward the back of the hook. Stop just at the bend, and then make a couple of wraps forward.

The Red Llama

Hook:	2X-long wet-fly hook, size 10 or 12.
Thread:	Black 8/0.
Tail:	Grizzly hackle fibers.
Body:	Red silk floss.
Rib:	Fine oval silver tinsel (or oval gold tinsel).
Wing:	Woodchuck hair.
Hackle:	Grizzly, tied as a collar.
Head:	Black, with painted yellow eyes with black pupils.

3. Strip the metallic covering from the end of a piece of fine oval tinsel, exposing the thread core. Hold the core against the hook and attach it with a wrap of tying thread.

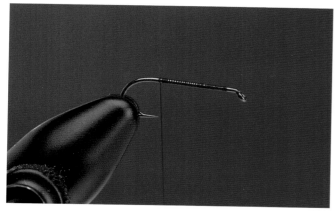

1. Attach the thread behind the hook eye. Cover the hook shank with thread wraps to the spot above and between the barb and the hook point. This is where you will attach the tail.

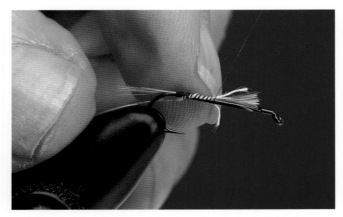

4. Continue to wrap the thread forward, binding the core of the tinsel and the butts of the tail to the hook. There should be a small gap between the base of the tail and the tie-in spot of the tinsel. This is for the first turn of floss when you begin to wrap the body.

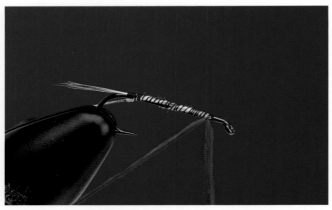

5. Stop about a hook-eye length behind the front of the shank, leaving room to attach the wing and hackle. Cut a length of red floss. Allow the bobbin to hang straight down. Hold the floss in your left hand, and bring one end of it around the far side of the thread. Pinch the two ends of the floss together behind the thread. Raise the bobbin to trap the floss against the hook shank. Make several wraps in front of the floss, around the hook shank only.

6. Let go of the short end of the floss and make a few wraps of thread toward the rear of the hook. Pull the long end of the floss to the rear, drawing the short end under the thread wraps. Then wind the thread back to where the tinsel is hanging, and forward again to the original tie-in spot.

7. Make the first wrap of floss in the gap between the base of the tail and the tinsel. Hold the tinsel out of the way, and then wrap the floss forward in front of it.

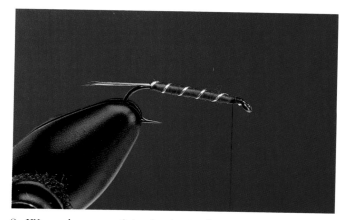

8. Wrap the rest of the body. Make sure to allow some overlap with each wrap. If you stroke the floss while wrapping, the strands will remain straight and taut, producing a smoother body. Make five equally spaced wraps of the tinsel toward the front of the hook. The last turn must end at the bottom of the hook shank. Secure the tinsel and clip the excess portion.

9. The best woodchuck hair is from an animal that had its winter coat. The underfur is thick and the guard hairs have just the right amount of color. These characteristics are what make this fly effective. When tying the Red Llama as a streamer, most of the underfur is removed and only the guard hairs are used. But since we are tying this one wet-fly style, we want the underfur in the wing.

10. Cut off enough hair for the wing. Remove all but ten of the guard hairs, leaving the underfur intact. Measure the wing; it should reach from just behind the hook eye to the bend of the hook. Cut the excess off the butt ends of the hair.

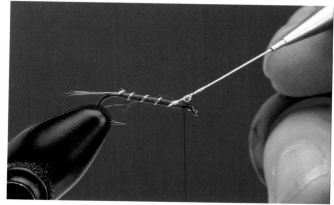

11. Apply a drop of cement to the thread at the tie-in spot for the wing. This cement will penetrate the wing from the bottom, helping to bond the hair to the hook.

12. Hold the wing in place with your left hand. Bring the thread over the butts of the hair and down on the far side of the hook. Tighten the thread by pulling the bobbin downward. Make another wrap and tighten it.

13. Finish securing the wing with additional wraps, forming the beginning of a head. Make your last wrap at the back of where the finished head will be.

14. Use a grizzly wet-fly hackle for this fly. The fibers should be about as long as the body. Strip the trash from the butt end of the hackle stem.

15. Attach the hackle by the butt end. Fold the stem to the rear and bind it down with thread, locking the feather in place. Clip the excess hackle stem and move the thread to just behind the hook eye.

16. Wrap the hackle toward the front of the hook, using as much as you need to make a full collar. Secure the feather and cut off the excess.

17. With your left hand, stroke the fibers to the rear of the fly and hold in place. Wrap the thread over the base of the hackle fibers, causing them to lie back. This should be right where the finished head will be. Build the head, half-hitch the thread, and apply cement.

18. Paint the eyes with lacquer. Whittle two wooden matchsticks to the sizes for the iris and the pupil. Paint the head of the fly with black lacquer and let it dry. Dip the larger matchstick in yellow lacquer and make an iris on each side of the head. Let the yellow paint dry before adding the pupil. Then dip the smaller matchstick in black lacquer and make a pupil in the center of each eye. Let the eyes harden overnight, and then add a coat of clear lacquer to protect them.

MORE THAN ONE WAY TO SKIN A LLAMA

Years ago, I ordered my fly-tying supplies from Eric Leiser. Eric is a household name among fly tiers. Show me a fly tier without Eric's *The Complete Book of Fly Tying,* and I will show you a fly tier who doesn't take his art seriously.

I always attached a fly to my order. Once, I sent a Red Llama with an order. When my materials arrived, the package contained a note from Eric pointing out that I was tying the fly wrong. Needless to say, I was a bit confused. After all, Miles Turtlelot himself had shown me how to tie the fly.

Eric had enclosed one of his Red Llamas. It was tied as a streamer, which was how Eric had learned the pattern. As I noted earlier, both the streamer and wet-fly styles are productive.

Years later, I was at a fly-tying demonstration and discovered that Eric was tying four chairs down the table from my spot. I walked up behind him and placed one

of my Red Llamas in front of him. Without turning around, Eric said, "Royce!" We met for the first time, after corresponding for eighteen years.

The Red Llama is also tied as a Yellow, Golden, or White Llama. Another very useful version is called the Hop Chuck. It's constructed like the Red Llama, but with green yarn or dubbing for the body. You've already learned how to tie the fly, so let's concentrate on painting the eyes, a trick you can use on many flies.

More Than One Way to Skin a Llama	
Hook:	1X-long wet-fly hook, size 8, such as a Daiichi 1560, Tiemco 3761, or Mustad 3906B.
Thread:	Black 12/0 (or black 6/0 or 8/0).
Tail:	Red hackle fibers (or a short piece of red yarn).
Body:	Green wool yarn (or green wool dubbing).
Wing:	Woodchuck hair.
Hackle:	Grizzly wet-fly hackle.
Head:	Black, with painted yellow eyes.

1. Tie the fly as you did the Red Llama. Paint the head with black lacquer and let it dry. Use a matchstick whittled to size to apply a dot of yellow lacquer on each side of the fly's head.

2. Let the yellow lacquer dry completely. Using a matchstick whittled to a point, apply a tiny dot of black lacquer to each eye.

3. Let the eyes dry overnight. A final coat of clear lacquer will keep the eyes from chipping.

THE GRIZZLY KING

This fly, another great old attractor pattern, demonstrates another method of making wings. We'll tie it first with wings made from the tips of hackle feathers. This version of the fly can also be tied as a streamer on a long-shank hook and with long hackle tips. The tail, floss body, rib, and hackle require techniques you've learned from previous flies in this chapter.

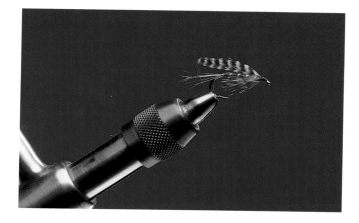

The Grizzly King

Hook:	1X-long wet-fly hook, size 8, such as a Daiichi 1560, Tiemco 3761, or Mustad 3906B.
Thread:	Black 10/0.
Tail:	Grizzly hackle fibers.
Body:	Green floss.
Rib:	Fine silver tinsel.
Hackle:	Grizzly saddle hackle.
Wing:	Two grizzly hackle tips.

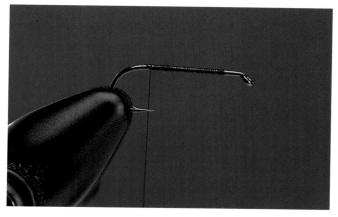

1. Attach the thread one hook-eye length behind the eye. Make side-by-side wraps to just above the point of the hook.

2. Measure the length of the tail material. The tail should be about as long as the fly's body.

3. Cut the excess material from the butts of the fibers.

4. Tie in the tail. Note that the butts are long enough to make a smooth underbody. Trimming the butts too short will create a lump.

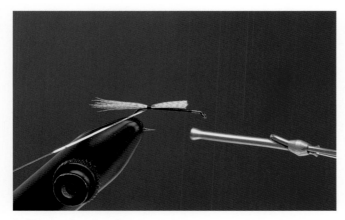

5. Tie in the tinsel.

6. Wind the thread forward, binding down the butts of the tail fibers. Loop a strand of green floss around the thread, as you did on the Red Llama.

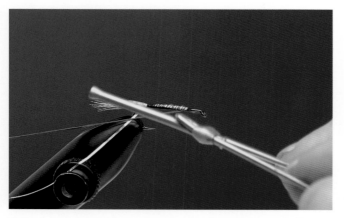

7. Raise the bobbin, trapping the floss against the hook. Make a few wraps in front of the floss, around the hook shank. Release the short end of the floss and make a few wraps of thread toward the rear of the hook. Pull on the long end of the floss, drawing the short end under the thread wraps.

8. Wind the thread almost to the spot where the tinsel is attached. Don't wrap all the way to the base of the tail; leave room for one turn of floss at the end of the hook shank.

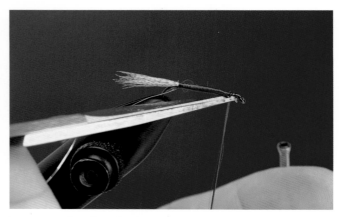

9. Wrap the floss body as you did on the Red Llama. Tie off the floss on the underside of the shank and clip the excess.

10. Make five evenly spaced turns with the ribbing tinsel. The third turn should be at the center of the fly. Tie off the tinsel beneath the hook shank.

11. Select a hackle that has fibers that will just about reach the point of the hook. Separate the hackle fibers at the tie-in spot near the tip of the hackle. By tying in the hackle at the tip, you will waste less material than if you tie it in at the butt end. When you attach the hackle, make sure that the shiny side is facing out.

12. Fold the hackle fibers to one side of the stem. Start winding the hackle, stroking the fibers to the rear and making each turn in front of the preceding one.

13. After several turns of hackle, make a wrap of thread over the stem to hold it in place. Fold the hackle stem to the rear, over the top of the hook. Gather the fibers and hold them to the rear while wrapping the thread over the base of the hackle. Try to make smooth thread wraps. You want a smooth foundation for the wings. Cut excess hackle, but save it; you might have enough left to hackle another fly.

14. Select a pair of matching feathers from a grizzly neck; a hen neck is a good choice. Make sure that the feathers have the same shape and markings.

15. Hold the butts of the two feathers together with your right index finger and thumb, and measure the length of the wings. The wings should reach to the bend of the hook.

17. Bind down the wing stems all the way to the eye of the hook. Clip any excess at the rear of the hook eye.

16. Cut the stems before tying the feathers in place. Tie the stems in place using the same techniques used when tying a hair wing. If the hackle stems want to roll as you tie them in, remove the feathers and flatten the stems with a smooth-jawed pliers.

18. Finish wrapping the Grizzly King's head, tie off the thread, and apply cement.

Many tiers make the Grizzly King with a wing of mallard-flank or wood-duck fibers. In fact, that's probably the more common way to tie it, so let's do it next. The tail, body, rib, and hackle are the same as on the hackle-tip version; only the wing material changes. For the example in the photos, I used wood duck.

2. Squeeze the feather between your fingers, rolling all the fibers on the tip into a neat bundle. Measure the length of the wing. The tips of the fibers should reach slightly beyond the bend of the hook.

1. Construct the tail, body, and hackle. Select a wood-duck flank feather with good markings and a fairly even shape.

3. Transfer the feather to your left hand, and cut off the excess portion, leaving the material you will use for the wing.

4. Hold the wing on top of the hook with the butts even with the back of the hook eye. At this point, we're treating the bundle of wood-duck fibers much like a clump of hair.

5. Tie the wing in place, shape the fly's head, and tie off the thread.

THE COLEMAN LAKE SPECIAL

This fly will show how to shape a body with wool dubbing. The wing is hair from the tail of a red fox squirrel. A similar pattern, called the Coleman Lake, has a wing of white calf hair; the only difference between the two flies is the wing material.

The Coleman Lake Special

Hook:	1X-long wet-fly hook, such as a Daiichi 1560, Tiemco 3761, Mustad 3906B, or Dai Riki 060.
Thread:	Black 12/0 (or black 6/0 or 8/0).
Tail:	Grizzly hackle fibers.
Body:	Gray wool dubbing (or heather-colored wool dubbing).
Wing:	Hair from a fox squirrel's tail (or from the tail of a pine squirrel).
Hackle:	Grizzly.

1. Prepare the wool dubbing. Separate a bundle of wool from the rest of the patch, and cut it as close to the hide as possible.

2. Place the clump of wool on one of your brushes. Put the other brush on top, making the "wool sandwich" described earlier, and work the brushes against each other to comb and card the wool.

3. You end up with a neat pile of dubbing, with all the wool fibers aligned.

4. Attach the thread to the hook, tie on the tail, and bind down the butts.

5. Pull a little wool from the brush by grabbing the tips of the fibers and drawing them away.

6. Attach the tips of the wool fibers to the thread. Remember always to twist in one direction, not back and forth.

7. Twist the fibers around the the thread until the tips are attached, as shown. For the moment, don't worry about the rest of the dubbing.

8. Start wrapping the dubbed thread around the hook shank. If you hold the bottom end of the dubbing and the thread together, the fibers will twist around the thread while you work.

9. Wrap to the rear until you reach the base of the tail. Then reverse direction and start wrapping forward. Maintain your grip on the thread and dubbing, and the material will continue to twist into a tight rope, as this has.

10. Finish winding the body, leaving room to attach the wing and hackle. The body should taper toward the front of the fly, like this one does.

11. Cut a clump of hair from the tail of a red squirrel. Clip the hair close to the skin.

12. Measure the length of the wing. It should extend beyond the bend of the hook, but not to the end of the tail.

13. Tie on the wing as you did on any of the other hair-wing flies in this chapter.

14. Attach the hackle feather and clip the excess stem.

15. Wind the hackle, stroking the fibers toward the rear of the fly as you make each turn. Tie off the hackle, finish the fly's head, and apply cement.

CHAPTER 3

Tying Dry Flies

Tying dry flies differs from tying wets. A dry fly is tied on a hook made of finer wire. The lengths of the tails, wings, bodies, and hackles are different on the two types of flies. A hackle feather for a dry has little, if any, web, and it comes from a rooster neck or saddle.

The parts of a dry fly are also made differently than those of wet flies. In this chapter, you will learn how to make divided wings, post wings, down wings, and spent wings. You will also learn how to wrap the hackles of divided-wing flies, parachute patterns, and down-wing caddisflies. Although you learned how to measure tails in the last chapter, you must be especially careful with the lengths of dry-fly tails. Most of the flies in this chapter have dubbed bodies, for which you will use the wool dubbing described earlier.

WHITE WULFFS AND WHITE WADERS

Late one spring, my longtime friend Lou Biscoff showed up at my door with fishing on his mind. Lou was on his way to the Yellowstone country. He had done his share of roughing it and wasn't as young as he used to be. So, instead of his trusty old tent, he had brought a camper with him. We talked about fishing and marveled at the comfort that his camper would provide, and decided to give it a try up on the Prairie River for a day or two before Lou moved on to chase cutthroats out West.

We found a great spot to park the camper on an old logging road lined with pine trees and oozing the living scent of spring. We set up a camp that would make any tourist proud, and then suited up for the stream. I was a little concerned about turning Lou loose in some of the faster water. The Prairie can get a little tough on us old timers. Like an old mother hen I put him in slow water, thinking he would be safer there. Lou didn't say a word. I walked up into some of the faster water and tied on a fly. Before I made my first cast I turned to check on my buddy. He had vacated the slow water for the more productive fast water and was already three quarters of a mile downstream.

It was late in the afternoon when we began fishing. That time of the year, dark sneaks up on you pretty quickly. Lou made his way back upstream in my direction. When we were within earshot of each other, I asked him how he had done. He said he had one nice fish follow the Hornberg he had started with, but that was all. On the way back to the camper we approached a fishy-looking spot at a sharp bend in the river. I asked Lou to hold up a minute. I wanted to try fishing a White Wulff.

I like fishing after dark better than at any other time. The big browns are nocturnal in nature, and they feed on larger insects and other critters that end up in the stream. We have a major Hex hatch on our streams in Wisconsin, and the browns, being opportunistic feeders, will take a good Hex imitation after dark. I put on a White Wulff tied on a size 8 salmon-fly hook.

When Lou saw the size of the fly I was tying on, he didn't say a word. The look of doubt on his face was enough. You need to dope up a dry fly that big with quite a bit of floatant to make it ride nicely on the surface. I always make the first cast or two at close range. This is a good idea for a couple of reasons. The first is to find out if there are any fish close to you and to avoid putting them down by casting over their backs. The second is to get a good idea of the speed of the current so that you can gauge where your fly is in the dark. I didn't have a taker on the two casts up close, so I stripped some line from my reel and laid one out in the dark.

I didn't have to feel the hit. The explosion in the water out in front of us was all I needed to set my hook. After a hearty fight, I guided the fish toward Lou so he could see the trout that huge fly had fooled. He did get a look at it before the brown gave one last violent shake of the head and broke free.

All the while Lou remained silent and curious. I tied on another White Wulff and proceeded to land two more nice browns in the nineteen-inch range. Shaking his head in disbelief, Lou decided it was time to head to the camper for some nourishment.

We grunted out of our waders and climbed into Lou's camper. The night air was a bit chilly and the warmth of the camper felt pretty darned good. I hung my waders just inside the door and Lou hung his on a light fixture just outside the door. I mentioned to him as he closed the door that he really ought to bring them inside because it gets pretty cold at night in the spring. He thought they would be just fine and began to cook up a pan of hot soup.

Lou doesn't mess around when he fixes supper. He poured into a pan two cans of soup, a can of corn, a can of lima beans, and a can of peas. I looked at the size of that kettle he was preparing and asked him if he was expecting company. "No," he explained. "We won't have any trouble eating this meager meal after a hard day of fishing."

With our bellies full of hot soup and cold beer we were ready to crawl into our sleeping bags for the night.

Lou turned one of the stove burners on low and opened a vent in the ceiling. We drifted off to sleep warm and cozy. This sure as hell does beat a tent, I thought to myself as I began to dream of big trout.

Early the next morning the beer from the night before was working on both of us, and we headed out the door. Just outside the door we both stopped in our tracks and started laughing. Lou's waders had changed colors during the night. They were as white as the hackle on a White Wulff. As I had warned, they were covered by a quarter-inch of frost. Lou would need a pot of coffee before climbing into those waders.

I suspect the next time Lou fishes Wisconsin in the spring, he will hang his waders on the inside at night. And maybe, if we fish after sunset, he'll try a White Wulff.

THE WHITE WULFF

This fly uses hair for its tail and wings. Calf-tail hair is the standard material, but elk, elk mane, or deer hair can also be used. When shopping for calf tails, look for those that have fairly even hair. Cut the hair from the tail as close to the hide as possible. With calf-tail or calf-body hair, it is a good idea to use a stacker to even the hairs at their tips. If the hairs on a tail are fairly even though, there is no need to stack them; on a larger fly, such as the one in the photographs, I think it's better to have the tips of the hairs a little uneven.

As in the patterns for wet flies, optional or substitute materials are listed in parentheses.

The White Wulff

Hook:	1X-long or 2X-long dry-fly hook (or a standard-length hook).
Thread:	White prewaxed 8/0.
Tail:	Calf-tail hair (or elk, elk mane, or body hair from a coastal or Texas deer).
Wing:	Calf-tail hair (or elk, elk mane, or body hair from a coastal or Texas deer).
Body:	White wool dubbing.
Hackle:	White saddle hackle.

1. Attach the thread at the one-third mark of the hook shank and wind it back toward the bend. Select a calf tail that has fairly straight hair.

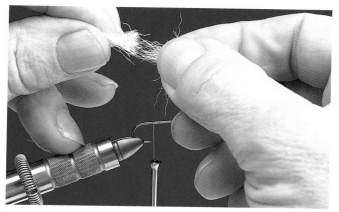

2. Cut a clump of hair with enough material for the tail. Hold the clump near the tips with your left hand, and clean out the short hairs with your right hand.

3. The tail measurement is from the front of the hook eye to the bend of the hook. If the tail is not long enough, the fly will roll on its side when you fish it. Grasp the hairs with your left thumb and index finger, marking the tie-in spot with your thumbnail. Place the hair above the last wrap of the thread. Before tying the hairs in, cut the butt ends at the one-third mark of the hook shank.

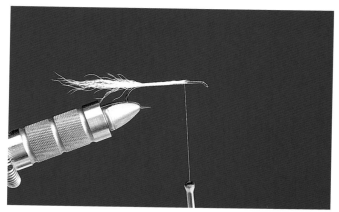

4. Make the first tie-down wraps toward the rear of the hook. After the first few wraps, reposition your grip near the tips of the hair. Hold the hairs at a slight angle to you, continuing the tie-down wraps. When you have reached the spot directly above the barb of the hook, reverse direction and wrap forward. Use the nail of your index finger as a guide; this will keep the hairs from rolling around the hook shank. Bind down all the butts, stopping where you first attached the thread to the hook.

5. Cut the amount of hair needed for the wing. Use a bunch of hair that is about twice the diameter of the wire of the hook shank. Remove the fuzz from the butt ends, then even the tips of the hair in a stacker. When you remove the hair from the stacker, the tips should be facing toward the front of the hook and the butts to the rear. Grasp the tips with your right index finger and thumb. Next, transfer the hair to your left hand for measuring. The measurement for the wing is from the point of the hook to the hook eye. Mark the tie-in spot with your left thumb and index finger.

6. Add a drop of cement at the tie-in spot on the hook. Hold the hair on top of the hook and make a half-dozen thread wraps to the rear.

7. Raise the butt ends off the hook and cut them at an angle to the tail. Continue wrapping to the rear, binding down the butts of the hair. Wrap all the way to the base of the tail.

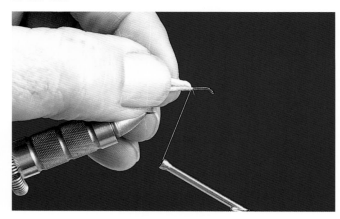

8. Return your thread to the first tie-in wraps of the wing. Grasp the hair with your left index finger and thumb and pull it tightly to the rear.

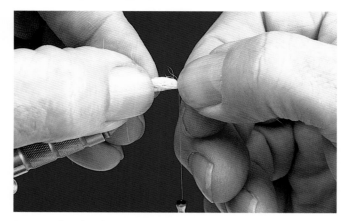

9. Divide the hair into two bunches by placing your right thumbnail at the base of the wing. While holding the hair tight, press against the base of the clump with your thumbnail to divide the wings.

10. With the wings divided, make thread wraps between the two bunches of hair. Grasp the wing nearer to you with your left thumb and index finger. Make two thread wraps between the wings, wrapping from the front of the near wing and passing the thread diagonally between the wings.

11. Now grasp the far wing with your left thumb and index finger and make two more thread wraps between the wings. Make these wraps from the back of the near wing to the front of the far wing. In other words, the thread passes over the hook diagonally from rear to front.

12. Add a drop of cement between the wings. This stiffens and reinforces the bases of the wings. Now you are ready to add the dubbing.

13. The dubbing is the carded wool described in chapter 2. Cut some white wool and put it on one of your wire pet brushes. Put the other brush on top, sandwiching the wool between the brushes. Work the brushes against each other to tease, separate, and align the wool fibers.

14. Remove the amount of wool needed to dub the fly by grasping the tips of the hairs with your right index finger and thumb. You don't need a lot of material; this pinch will dub a dry fly.

15. Attach the tips of the wool to the thread as close to the hook shank as possible, using a counterclockwise twisting motion. Once the tips of the fibers are attached, make one turn of the wool dubbing around the hook shank, trapping the dubbing between the thread and the hook. Then hold the bobbin with your left hand, and, with the thread tight, grasp the lower end of the dubbing and the thread. Stretch the dubbing a little, and twist it around the thread between your right index finger and thumb. Use a rolling motion to attach the dubbing. Once the dubbing is attached at both ends, twist the rest onto the thread.

16. Grasp the thread and the dubbing and cradle the bobbin at the butt of your hand. Start to wrap the dubbing around the hook, shaping the body as you go. As you wrap dubbing, always keep the opening of your index finger and thumb facing the hook shank. When you reach the wings, gently pull them rearward and wrap some dubbing in front of them.

17. Stop dubbing one and a half hook-eye lengths behind the hook eye. The dubbed area in front of and behind the wings will make a good foundation for the fly's hackle, which comes next.

18. Select a pair of saddle hackles. Remove the unusable part from the butt end of each. Hold the first hackle with your left hand with the good side of the feather facing up. Bind the stem of the feather securely to the hook, and then do the same with the second feather.

19. Wrap the hackle that's nearer to the wings first. Make two turns of hackle in front of the wings. Then make one turn behind them. Return to the front of the wings and make three wraps, the last of which ends in front of the second hackle. Tie off the first feather.

20. Make a couple of turns of the second hackle in front of the wings, then three turns behind the wings. As you make the third wrap of hackle behind the wings, bring the feather forward. Now use the rest of the hackle to fill in at the front of the fly. Tie off the second feather, half-hitch the thread, and cement the head.

WINDING TWO HACKLES

Larger dry flies and those fished in rough water often need heavy hackle collars made with two feathers. Some patterns, such as the popular Adams, use two hackles of different colors; this is called a mixed hackle. The next fly, a hairwing version of the Adams, shows a good technique for making a mixed hackle. You can use this method on just about any fly that uses two hackles of different colors. We'll pick up the sequence at the point of attaching the first hackle. Here's the recipe for the entire fly.

Hairwing Adams

Hook:	Standard dry-fly hook, sizes 4 to 12.
Thread:	Black 14/0.
Tail:	Elk mane.
Wings:	Woodchuck hair.
Body:	Gray wool dubbing.
Hackles:	One grizzly and one dyed-brown grizzly, from either a neck or a saddle.

1. Attach one hackle behind the wings. Leave enough space between the hackle and the wings for one turn of the feather.

2. Wind the thread to the front, stopping one and a half hook-eye lengths behind the eye. Tie in the second hackle.

3. Begin with the front hackle. Make one turn in front of the wings, one behind the wings, and then another two turns in front of the wings.

4. Tie off the feather and cut away the leftover part.

5. Now wrap the rear feather. Make one turn behind the wings, then bring the hackle in front of the wings and make two more wraps. Try to make these wraps in be-tween the turns of the first hackle you wrapped; you don't want to mash down any of the fibers.

6. Tie off the hackle and finish the fly's head.

THE LIGHT CAHILL SPARKLE DUN

This version of the Light Cahill uses Antron sparkle yarn for the tail rather than the standard clump of hackle fibers. Sometimes, a hatching mayfly cannot get rid of its nymphal shuck, and a piece of sparkle yarn makes a good imitation of a shuck trailing behind an insect struggling to emerge. Attaching a trailing shuck requires no special techniques; simply substitute a piece of sparkle yarn for a hackle-fiber or hair tail. The main lesson with this pattern is the technique for making wings with barred wood-duck feathers.

The Light Cahill Sparkle Dun

Hook:	Standard dry-fly hook, sizes 14 through 18.
Thread:	Light brown 8/0.
Tail:	Cream sparkle yarn.
Wings:	Wood-duck flank feathers.
Body:	Pale yellow wool dubbing.
Hackle:	Ginger.

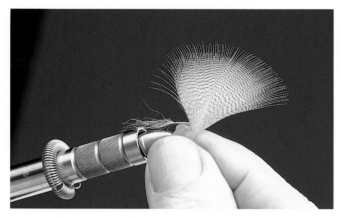

1. Start the thread a third of the way back from the hook eye, and cover the shank to the spot between the point and barb of the hook. Tie in a piece of sparkle yarn for the tail. Wind the thread forward to the original tie-in spot. Select two matched wood-duck flank feathers. Hold the feathers side by side to align the tips of the fibers.

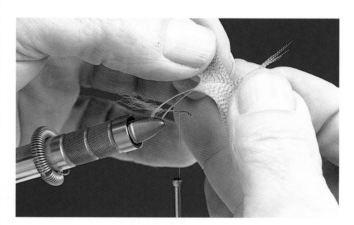

2. Strip the unusable fluff from the bases of the feathers. Remove the amount of material you will need for the wings. As you strip the fibers from the stems, take care to keep the tips aligned.

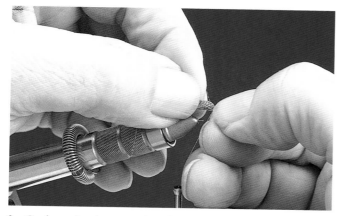

3. Gather the butt ends of the fibers and transfer the clump to your left hand for measuring. The wings' height should equal the distance from the point of the hook to the front of the hook eye. Tie the wing fibers in place with the tips pointing forward. Divide the bunch into two smaller clumps with your thumbnail, and then use diagonal wraps of thread to keep the wings separated, just as you did when making the hair wings on the White Wulff.

4. Dub the fly's body with yellow wool. Be sure to wrap some dubbed thread in front of the wings. Stop one hook-eye length from the front of the shank.

5. Tie in the hackle. Make a total of eight turns: two in front of the wings, three behind them, and then another three in front of the wings. As you bring the feather in front of the wings, try to make the wraps between those you made earlier, not on top of them. The final wrap of hackle is just in front of the first turn. Tie off the feather, clip the left-over part, and finish the fly's head.

THE PALE MORNING DUN PARACHUTE

Parachutes have long been popular with fly fishers. The differences between this pattern and those we've already tied are the wing, which is a single clump of hair, and the hackle, which is applied horizontally rather than vertically.

The Pale Morning Dun Parachute

Hook:	Standard dry-fly hook, sizes 12 through 20.
Thread:	Light brown 8/0.
Tails:	Hackle fibers.
Wing:	Calf body hair.
Body:	Pale yellow wool dubbing, made by mixing yellow with gray or brown.
Hackle:	Light Cree neck or saddle feather.

1. Start the thread a little behind the one-third mark of the shank and wind back to just behind the point. Tie in the tail. Advance the thread to the original tie-on spot. Cut a clump of calf hair for the wing; use about half as much as you would on a divided-wing fly. Stack the hairs to even the tips. Establish the length of the wing; the measurement is from the point of the hook to the eye. Tie the wing clump in place with the tips pointing forward.

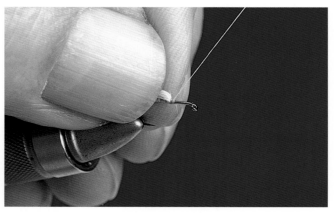

2. To stand the wing up, make several turns of the thread in front of it while holding the hair upright.

3. With the wing upright, make one clockwise wrap around the base, wrap once around the hook shank, and then make a counterclockwise wrap around the base of the wing. This will give you the same pressure on both sides of the wing. After wrapping the base of the wing, return the thread to the center of the body.

4. Dub the body. Stop at the very front of the wing, and form a small ball of dubbing there.

5. Strip the fibers from part of the hackle stem. Make one wrap of thread around the stripped hackle stem and the hook shank.

6. Bring the thread in front of the hackle stem and make one wrap around the hook shank only.

7. Make another few wraps of thread around both the hackle stem and the hook shank, working toward the eye of the hook.

8. Break off the piece of feather you don't need. Wind the thread back to the dubbing at the front of the wing. Twist a little more dubbing onto the thread, leaving a length of bare thread.

9. Start your turns of hackle around the wing, making clockwise wraps as viewed from above.

10. After three or four turns, stop on the far side of the hook. Grasp the tip of the feather with your right hand. Bring the feather toward you, going over the top of the shank, and underneath the thread.

11. Fold the hackle tip back.

12. Stroke the hackle fibers out of the way. Make several turns of thread toward the wing, binding the folded-back hackle stem to the hook.

13. While holding the hackle fibers out of the way, wrap a little dubbing in front of the wing, completing the fly's thorax. Once you have applied the dubbing, you can half-hitch the thread.

14. Remove the excess hackle tip by cutting it or by breaking it off by pulling it sharply toward the rear of the fly. Add a little cement to the head and at the base of the wing.

DAM'S HAIRWING CADDISFLY

I was tying flies in a shop in Brule, Wisconsin, when a wild-looking, bearded gentleman strolled in and asked if a guy named Royce Dam was around. I didn't know whether to run or sit tight. The owner of the shop pointed in my direction and said, "That'll be him sitting at the desk tying up some flies." I didn't realize it at the time, but this was the beginning of a great adventure.

The gentleman who sauntered up to me was Jack McGee. Jack had been camping and fishing on the Brule for more than a week, which explained his wild appearance. He asked if I was interested in going fishing with him. It was the start of a lifelong friendship.

Time passed. One weekend years later, I was assisting Gary Borger with a fly-casting workshop when Gary asked if I had ever fished the Yellowstone River. After I explained to him that even if money did grow on trees, I certainly didn't own one of the magic shrubs, Gary mentioned the idea of car pooling and splitting the cost. The trip started to sound possible. I thought of my old friend Jack McGee, and gave him a call to see if he would be interested in making the trip.

Jack was a pilot and flew a cargo plane for a company just outside of Milwaukee. He was pretty excited about the trip and took my idea one step further. "Why not fly out and split the cost of the fuel?" he asked. Everyone agreed, and the trip was on. Gary still planned to drive out and left a few days before we did, agreeing to pick us up at the airport when we arrived.

You need to understand that I had never flown before, not even when I was in the Marines. This trip meant enough to me that I was willing to put up with just about anything. But when I saw what we were flying in, my nerves began to have second thoughts. A small, three-passenger plane didn't do much to inspire confidence in a safe arrival. But Jack is such a comedian that he kept me in stitches throughout the trip, and kept my mind off our probable, premature deaths. We made it safely.

Gary picked us up at the airport. As we drove through the Yellowstone country toward the campsite, I marveled at the beauty around me. Northern Wisconsin has a wild beauty all its own, but the mountain peaks out West were breathtaking. Steam rose from thermal vents in the ground, elk crossed the road in front of us, and buffalo dotted the meadows. It was an ancient world, full of promise.

We feverishly set up camp in hopes of cheating the sun out of some fishing time. Gary loaded us up in the van for the short trip to the Yellowstone River. When we pulled into the parking lot, the wheels of the van had barely stopped before the side door opened and anglers poured out like angry bees from a hive.

Since this was my first trip to the Yellowstone, I decided to take some time to observe the environment. While everyone else was assembling rods and grunting their way into tight-fitting waders, I watched and learned. I grabbed a few of the flying insects to see what the fish were continuously rising to. Darkness finally drove everyone out of the water and back to the van.

When we arrived at camp, I pulled out my travel pack of tying tools and materials. In the absence of a tying table and light, I used the glove box lid and light in Gary's van to tie a couple of caddisflies for each of us to fish the next morning. The flies were small, size 18 or 20. Their size made tying them in poor light and on the glove box lid a major undertaking, but I managed to get the job done. With the difficult working conditions, I had to make the pattern simple. The morning would offer proof of the flies' effectiveness, or lack thereof. I slept well and dreamed of native Yellowstone cutthroats dancing on the end of my line.

Morning came none too soon. I rationed out the new patterns to each of my buddies. We had a quick breakfast and made our way to the stream. The fly was a fish charmer. Well before noon, I had landed forty-five trout. Before the day was over, each of us had netted at least a hundred fish. Those rare days are the ones that set like concrete in your memory.

This magic little fly is the next one we'll tie. If you are headed for Yellowstone, be sure to tie up a dozen or more before leaving home. They worked well on other streams on the same trip and have worked well since.

Many years later, Gary asked me if I remembered that hundred-fish day on the Yellowstone. Who could forget?

Dam's Hairwing Caddisfly

Hook:	Standard dry-fly hook, sizes 12 through 20.
Thread:	Black 8/0.
Body:	Light brown wool dubbing.
Wing:	Deer or elk body hair.
Hackle:	Grizzly.

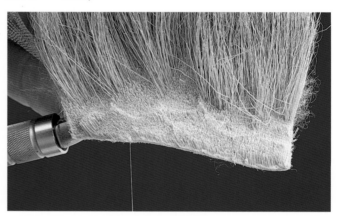

1. Attach the thread and wind it back to the end of the hook shank. Prepare some wool dubbing and make the body. The wing of the fly is made of body hair from a white-tailed deer. You'll want a patch of skin with fairly fine hair.

2. Cut a small clump of hair from the skin. Tie the hair at the front of the body. Use the tip of your left index finger to keep the hair in place as you tie it in.

4. Lift the butts of the hair and cut them. Bind down the butts with wraps of thread.

3. The tips of the wing should reach beyond the bend of the hook.

5. Attach and wind the hackle. Tie off the hackle feather and finish the fly's head.

A TENT-WING CADDIS

The next fly is also a caddis, but it has a refinement that makes it more realistic. The wing consists of two materials: a sparse clump of elk or deer hair with a goose-quill section "tented" over the top and trimmed to shape.

Tent-Wing Caddis

Hook:	Standard dry-fly hook, sizes 14 through 20.
Thread:	Black 8/0.
Body:	Light brown wool dubbing.
Wing:	Dyed-black elk or deer hair, and a piece of dyed-black goose quill.
Hackle:	Grizzly, dyed dark dun.

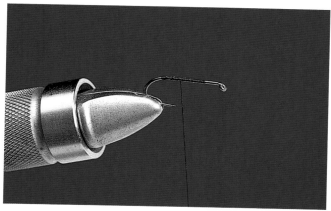

1. Start the thread one hook-eye length behind the eye and wrap back to just above the barb. Return the thread to the center of the shank.

2. Begin the body at the center of the hook. Twist some dubbing onto the thread, and wrap the dubbed thread first to the rear, and then to the front. The body should have a tapered shape, thicker at the rear. Dub the body all the way to the original tie-on wraps, one hook-eye length behind the front of the shank.

3. Cut a small clump of black deer or elk hair. Stack the hair to even the tips, and measure the wing from the hook eye to the bend of the hook.

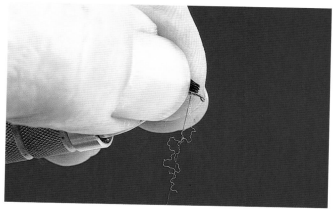

4. Cut the hair to length. Add a little head cement to the spot where the wing will be attached. Tie the hair in place.

5. Shape the head before adding the quill-slip overwing.

6. Cut a section from a dyed-black goose quill that has been treated with clear Krylon coating. The quill section should be wide enough to cover the top of the fly.

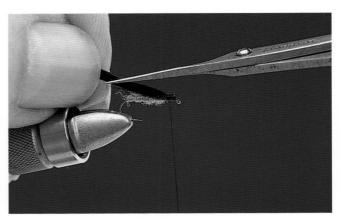

7. Cup the quill section on top of the fly and tie it in place. Shape the head and return the thread to the rearmost wrap of the thread at the base of the wing.

8. Pinch the quill section to fold it lengthwise. Cut the rear of the wing at an angle.

9. Make two or three turns of the hackle at the rear of the head. Tie off and clip the hackle feather. Finish the head, half-hitch the thread, and apply a drop of cement.

THE SPENT-WING RUSTY SPINNER

This pattern, an imitation of a spent mayfly, will show you how to use synthetic filaments for the tail and synthetic yarn for the wing. The tail fibers go under several brand names; Microfibetts is probably the most popular. For the wing, you can use polypropylene yarn (the most common material), Antron yarn, sparkle yarn, or a product called Z-Lon. The techniques used for the tails and the wing are different from those you have seen so far. You will use these techniques to tie just about any spent mayfly pattern.

The Spent-Wing Rusty Spinner

Hook:	Standard dry-fly hook, sizes 16 through 22.
Thread:	Dark brown 8/0.
Tail:	Reddish brown Microfibetts or similar material.
Wing:	Poly yarn or sparkle yarn.
Body:	Rust-colored wool dubbing.

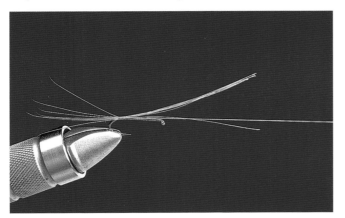

1. Wrap the hook shank with thread. At the very rear of the shank, wind a small ball of thread. Attach several Microfibetts with a few wraps of thread. The tails on this fly are quite long; they should measure almost twice the length of the hook shank.

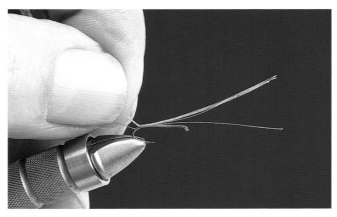

2. Lift the tail filaments and bring the thread under them.

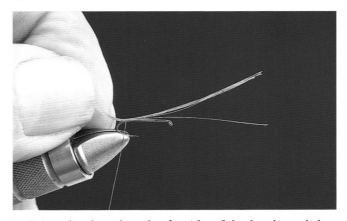

3. Bring the thread to the far side of the hook, and then pull it forward to tighten the wrap behind the tails. This raises and separates the tail fibers.

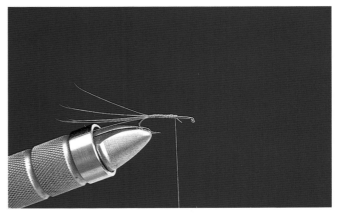

4. Continue binding the butts of the tail filaments to the hook. Cut off the excess. Stop where shown, about a third of the way back on the shank.

5. Cut a piece of polypropylene yarn or sparkle yarn. Make the yarn long enough so that it's easy to handle; you will trim it later. Hold the yarn on top of the hook, with the middle of the piece over the tying thread. Make one wrap around the yarn.

6. Grab the rear end of the yarn and pull it to the far side of the hook so that the piece is roughly perpendicular to the shank. Make a couple of diagonal wraps of thread, angled from back to front.

7. Make another couple of diagonal wraps of thread, this time angled from front to rear. The point is to bind the yarn across the hook with an X of thread.

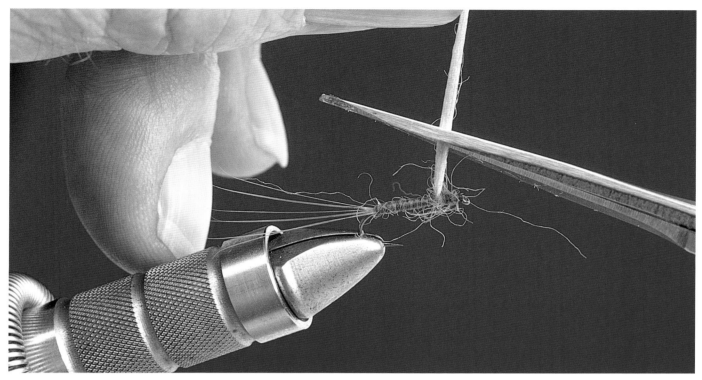

8. Apply dubbing to the thread. Dub the fly's body, and make a thorax around the wings. After dubbing the body, tie off the thread. Lift both wings and cut them to length. Put a drop of cement on the head.

THE ARROWHEAD

The Arrowhead is tied as a high-floating, easily seen bivisible fly. It uses two hackles, the tips of which become tails. The body is made of peacock herl twisted in a loop of thread to make it more durable.

The Arrowhead	
Hook:	Standard dry-fly hook, sizes 10 through 14.
Thread:	8/0.
Body:	Peacock herl.
Tail:	The tips of the hackles.
Hackle:	One grizzly and one brown.

1. Attach the thread one hook-eye length behind the eye. Wrap back to the bend, and then forward to the middle of the shank. Tie in the tip ends of two pieces of peacock herl.

2. Wrap the herl around the tying thread. Hold the butt ends of the herl and the thread together.

3. While holding the butt ends of the herl and the thread, bring the bobbin over the hook and make one wrap of thread around the shank. Then wind the thread forward to within a hook-eye length of the front of the shank. You will have made a loop of thread, with the peacock herl twisted around one side of the loop.

4. Twist the loop of thread, trapping the peacock herl. This reinforces the herl and makes for a very durable body. Wrap the twisted herl around the hook. Wrap to the rear first, then forward to where the thread is hanging.

5. Tie off the herl and cut the excess.

6. Spiral the thread through the peacock herl until you reach the end of the body. Select two hackle feathers, one brown and one grizzly.

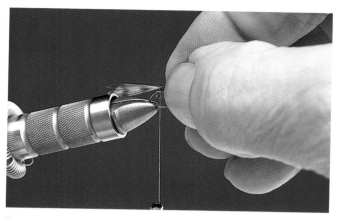

7. Separate the hackle fibers at the tie-in spot. Hold the hackles above the hook with the tips pointing to the rear.

8. Attach the hackles with a couple of wraps of thread.

9. Lift the hackles out of the way and spiral the thread forward through the body. Wind the brown hackle first, leaving enough space between the wraps so that you can wrap the grizzly feather. Tie off the brown hackle, and then wrap the grizzly. Tie off the grizzly hackle and finish the fly's head. As you tie off each feather, use the locking system described earlier.

THE BROWN DRAKE: "ONLY ENOUGH FOR MYSELF!"

Back in August of 1990, the Federation of Fly Fishers had their annual conclave in Eugene, Oregon. My good friend Lou Biscoff and I had talked about making the trip together. Lou was going to drive up to Alaska for some fishing after the conclave. I wouldn't be able to make the Alaska trip, so I planned to drive out with him and then fly back.

Since Lou was going to fish Alaska, I decided to fix him up with a couple of handfuls of Brown Drakes. That time of the year, hitting a hatch was a good probability.

We made arrangements to meet up with a couple of Lou's friends in Yellowstone, where we would backpack five miles into the high country. Looking back on that decision, I realize I must have been out of my mind. I hadn't carried a pack since I was in the Marines. I was pushing sixty-five years of age. They say that age is only a state of mind. So I thought, until that trip.

When we arrived in Yellowstone, the daytime temps were hitting ninety degrees. The heat alone was a bit much for my constitution, but we also had to contend with the lack of oxygen at that altitude. Halfway to our destination, I had to 'fess up that my back, feet, and lungs were on fire. Gasping for air, I dropped my pack and told my friends to bury me were I sat. After taking much ribbing and name-calling, including a comment about the "old woman of the tribe," I summoned the strength and will power to make the rest of the trip.

We found a great spot to set up camp right next to the river and set about doing all of the things you do when you set up camp. We pitched the tent, hung the food in a tree to keep the grizzly bears out of it, and laid out our sleeping bags. You know how they say on the box, "This tent sleeps four"? I believe what they are referring to is four gnomes.

When you reach a certain age you find that you have to get up in the middle of the night a couple of times. Just my luck, I got stuck at the back of the tent, where I had to crawl over three other people to make my nightly runs. I hoped the fishing would be worth all the inconvenience.

The fishing was fair. Well, for most of us it was. One evening a nice brown-drake hatch came off. Lou was having a blast with the flies I had given him to fish in Alaska. None of the rest of us had a Brown Drake in our boxes. After sullenly watching Lou catch one nice fish after another, I swallowed my pride and hollered over to him, "Hey, Lou, how about a couple of those flies I gave you?"

Lou hooked another nice trout, turned to me with a devilish grin on his face, and replied, "Sorry, Royce, I only have enough for myself." Perhaps he was recalling a night on the Prairie River when I was catching big browns while he watched in envy. I don't know for sure, but I think he had more fun heckling the rest of us than he did fishing. Lou just loves to be the one on the front end of a good teasing.

Someday, Lou. Paybacks are hell.

In spite of the humiliation, the trip was a great one. Fishing with Lou still remains one of my favorite things to do.

The Brown Drake that Lou used with such success is tied just like the White Wulff, the first fly in this chapter. Here's the pattern.

The Brown Drake

Hook:	1X-long or 2X-long dry-fly hook (or a standard-length hook).
Thread:	Orange 8/0 (the thread will darken when the head cement is applied to it).
Tail:	Elk mane.
Wings:	Elk mane.
Body:	A blend of brown and yellow wool dubbing.
Hackle:	Brown saddle hackle.

The Brown Drake.

THE LITTLE GREEN BEETLE

Y ou can fish this pattern beneath the surface like a nymph, or on top like a dry fly. Since most anglers think of terrestrials as dry flies, I've put the beetle in this chapter. For a wet version, use a nymph hook, which is shown in the photos. To tie a floating beetle, use a standard dry-fly hook and treat the fly with floatant.

The Little Green Beetle

Hook:	Dry-fly or nymph hook, such as a Daiichi Hook No. 1180, size 18.
Thread:	Gray.
Legs:	Moose mane.
Shell:	Bright green rabbit fur.
Body:	Bright green wool dubbing.
Head:	The butts of the rabbit fur.

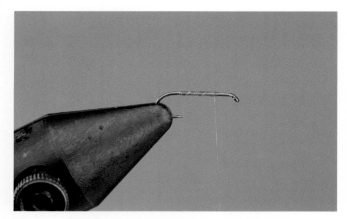

1. Wrap the hook shank with thread. Finish with the thread hanging about one hook-eye length behind the front of the shank.

2. Cut and stack a small clump of moose body hair. Attach the hair at the front of the hook, with the tips pointing forward. Trim the butts and wrap over them with thread.

3. Cut a piece of bright chartreuse rabbit strip with fur long enough to go over the top of the fly. Leave the fur attached to the hide. Moisten the fur, trim the tips so that they're even, and tie in the piece as shown, with the skin hanging off the back of the hook.

4. Dub the body with bright green wool.

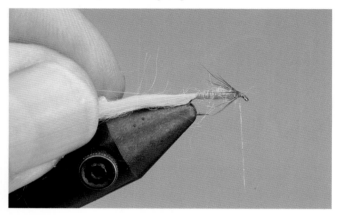

5. Divide the moose hairs into two equal clumps. Keep the bunches separated with diagonal wraps of thread and a tiny drop of cement. Grasp the piece of rabbit hide.

6. Fold the rabbit fur forward over the top of the fly. Tie down the fur just in front of the legs. After making a few wraps, raise the fur to get it out of the way and make a few more wraps behind the eye of the hook.

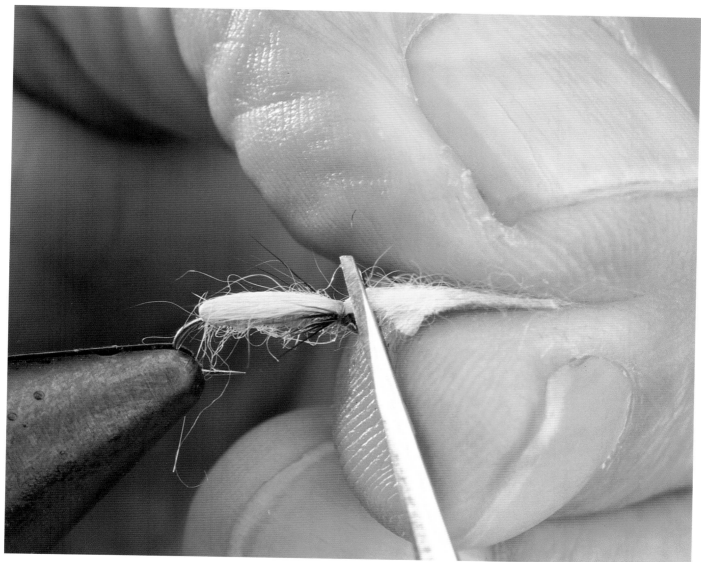

7. Tie off the thread. Cut the rabbit fur just ahead of the wraps holding it down. Apply a drop of cement to the head.

CHAPTER 4

Tying Nymphs

Tying nymphs will teach you how to use different materials for tails, wing cases, and legs. All of the nymphs in this chapter use wool dubbing in their bodies, though some use additional materials. You will notice that I generally don't use lead wire in my nymphs.

Rather than tie weight into my flies, I prefer to add it to my tippet, allowing the nymph to drift freely. The first fly, the Large Brown Stonefly, is the only one tied with lead wire.

THE LARGE BROWN STONEFLY

On this large nymph, I use wool dubbing as an underbody to shape the fly. This is the only fly in this chapter on which I use strips of lead wire, both to add weight and to give the bottom of the body a flattened shape. The fly's wing cases are made of folded pieces from a turkey quill.

The Large Brown Stonefly

Hook:	Daiichi Alec Jackson Spey hook, size 1.5 or 3 (or a similarly shaped salmon-fly hook).
Thread:	Brown 8/0.
Underbody:	Brown wool dubbing and strips of lead wire.
Tails:	Brown goose or turkey biots.
Back:	Dark brown raffia.
Abdomen:	Brown wool dubbing.
Rib:	Fine copper wire.
Thorax:	Amber wool dubbing.
Wing cases:	Sections from a turkey quill.
Legs:	Moose-body hairs.

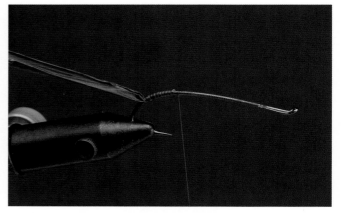

1. Start the thread two hook-eye lengths behind the eye and cover the hook shank to a spot above the point. Tie in a strip of dark brown raffia.

74

2. Twist some wool dubbing onto the thread and dub the underbody. Spiral the thread back to the rear of the hook. Tie in the ribbing wire, leaving enough room behind the wire to make one wrap of dubbed thread.

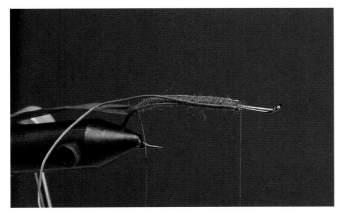

3. Tie strips of lead on each side of the underbody. This will make the body wider and flatter, along with adding weight to the fly. Attach one piece of wire on each side of the fly, add a strip on top of each of those, and then, between the first two strips, tie in a third piece on each side. Finally, attach a piece of flat lead along the top of the underbody.

4. Tie in the tails along the sides of the underbody. They should be no more than a quarter of an inch long. Twist some brown wool dubbing onto the thread and form the fly's abdomen. As you start to dub the abdomen, be sure to make one wrap of dubbing behind the ribbing wire.

5. Bring the raffia over the top of the fly and hold it down. Wind the ribbing wire forward in a spiral. Tie off the wire when you reach the front of the abdomen. Clip the leftover raffia and wire.

6. Cut two sections from a turkey quill to be used for the wing cases. Tie in the first wing case against the front of the abdomen. Twist amber wool dubbing onto the thread and dub the thorax. Add a little cement to the dubbing that the wing case will rest on. Fold the wing case forward over your bodkin, as shown.

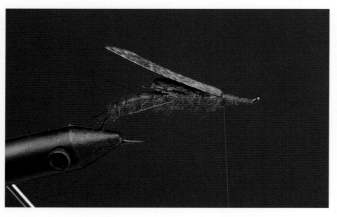

7. Tie down the first wing case. In this photo, you can see how it is folded. Clip the excess quill section, and then tie in the second wing case.

8. Use eight moose-body hairs for the legs. Place the hairs on top of the tie-in wraps of the second wing case. The legs should be fairly long.

9. Bind down the butts of the hairs securely. Don't clip the butts yet; you will take care of them in another couple of steps.

10. Divide the legs with your thumbnail into two equal bunches of four hairs. Add a little cement to the thread wraps.

11. Fold the second wing case over your bodkin. The second wing case is folded just ahead of the fold in the first one.

12. Keep the legs on the sides of the thorax as you fold the second wing case and bring it down to the head of the fly.

14. After securing the second wing case, cut the leftover quill section and the butts of the legs.

13. Tie down the second wing case. You can see how the legs come out from beneath the quill section on each side of the thorax.

15. Shape the head, half-hitch the thread, and add cement. You can also coat the wing cases if you wish; this will make the fly more durable.

DESIGNING THE LITTLE YELLOW STONEFLY

It was August and time to head for the Federation of Fly Fishers national conclave in West Yellowstone. I had been invited once again to demonstrate my fly-tying techniques. A couple of friends were driving out with me to help cut travel expenses.

One cannot attend an FFF conclave and not come away renewed and ready to fish. You spend a week discovering new materials and suppliers, seeing old friends, and comparing fishing stories from the past year. You have the opportunity to sit across a table from the best fly tiers in the world and watch them do their magic with feathers and fur. They are always ready and eager to share their knowledge and skills with you. If you are a serious fly fisher and have never attended one of these events, you owe it to yourself to make it to the next one.

After the conclave, a couple of friends and I decided to fish the Big Horn on the way home. We headed downriver, and, as most anglers do, I separated myself from the rest and began to observe what was going on in the trout's world. Black caddisflies were hatching, and the trout were hungrily rising to them. As I stood there watching the insects, I noticed something larger and lighter in color flying in my direction. Taking off my hat, I scooped it out of the air to see what it was. A small stonefly about three-quarters of an inch long was crawling around in the crown of my hat. The fly had light brown wings laid back over a pale yellow body. The lower part of the abdomen was reddish orange in color. Like any serious fly tier, I was already tying this fly in my mind. I kept imagining the larval or nymph stage and was designing the nymph pattern. I couldn't wait to get to my vise that evening to see what I could do.

The next morning I shared the novel-looking pattern with my friends. What a day we had. I remember standing in one spot and catching and releasing twenty-five to thirty fish on the Little Yellow Stonefly Nymph. The pattern below is exactly as I tied it those many years ago, and it's as effective as it was that day on the Big Horn. Give it a try.

The Little Yellow Stonefly

Hook:	4X-long nymph hook, size 14 or 16.
Thread:	Light brown 8/0.
Butt:	Bright red wool dubbing.
Tail:	Amber goose biots.
Rib:	Extra fine silver wire.
Body:	Pale yellow wool dubbing.
Wing case:	Brown raffia or a section from a turkey quill.
Thorax:	Pale yellow wool dubbing.
Legs:	Light elk-body hair.

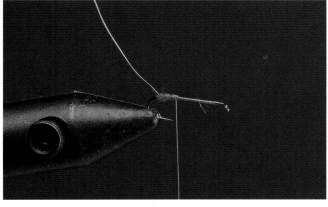

1. Start the thread one hook-eye length behind the eye. Cover the hook with thread wraps to the spot just above the point. Tie in the ribbing wire and add a small amount of red dubbing.

2. Attach a tail to each side of the hook shank, just in front of the butt. Be sure that the concave side of each tail faces out, so that the tails curve out from the hook. Add a little more red dubbing to the butt.

3. Use pale yellow wool to dub the abdomen, tapering the front of the body. Rib the body with evenly spaced turns of wire. Tie off the wire.

4. Tie on the quill section or raffia for the wing case. Bring the tie-down wraps back to the center of the body. Add more dubbing to the thread and make the thorax. This dubbing doesn't have to be very tight; you will pick it out later to make the thorax a little shaggier.

7. Lift the butt ends of the legs and wing case, and make a couple of turns of thread in front of them. Then make another few wraps where you originally tied down the wing case.

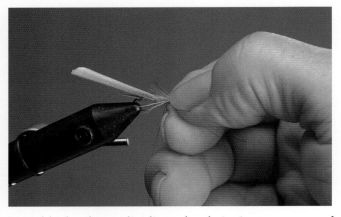

5. Add the legs, dividing the hair into two equal bunches. The hairs should extend a little past the wing case, to about the center of the abdomen.

8. Cut away the waste portions of the wing case and legs.

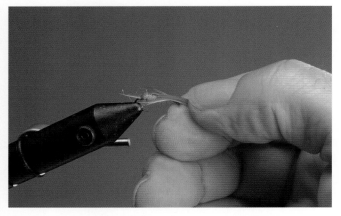

6. Make a couple of thread wraps over the separation point of the hairs. Bring the wing case forward and tie it down. The legs grow out of the thorax beneath the wing case.

9. Finish shaping the head. Half-hitch the thread and cement the fly's head.

THE SPECIAL HEX

This pattern imitates the nymph of the big Hex mayfly that's so important in the Midwest, and those of the green and brown drakes found in many parts of the country.

The Special Hex	
Hook:	1X-long wet-fly hook, size 6 (or a 2X-long hook in sizes 6 through 10, or a 3X-long in size 10 or 12).
Thread:	Brown 8/0.
Tail:	Wood-duck flank (or dyed mallard flank).
Back:	Ringneck-pheasant tail fibers.
Rib:	Copper wire.
Abdomen:	Grayish brown wool dubbing.
Wing case:	Turkey-quill slip.
Thorax:	Grayish brown wool dubbing.
Legs:	Partridge hackle (or wood-duck flank).

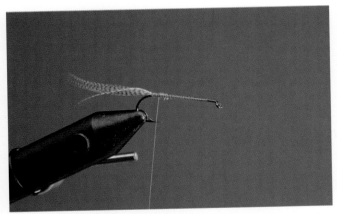

1. Attach the thread and wind it back to the spot between the point and barb. Strip about ten fibers from a
wood-duck feather. Measure the length of the tail; it
should be as long as the hook shank. Tie the tail in
place.

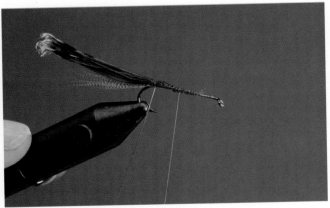

2. Strip some fibers from a pheasant tail. You'll need
enough to cover the top of the fly's abdomen. Tie in the
fibers by their tips with four or five wraps of thread. Attach the wire for the rib.

3. Dub the body. Wrap the dubbed thread from the
middle of the hook to the rear, make one turn behind
the ribbing wire, and then come forward. Stop dubbing
one and a half hook-eye lengths behind the eye.

4. Fold the pheasant fibers over the top of the abdomen.
Tie them down with a couple of wraps of thread. Wind
the rib, spacing the wraps a little farther apart as you
move forward. Tie off the wire.

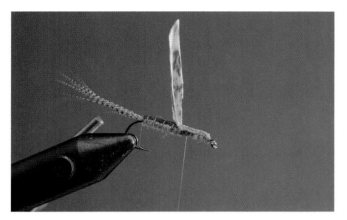

5. Cut the butts of the pheasant fibers. Wind the thread back to the center of the body. Prepare a section from a turkey quill wide enough to cover the thorax. Tie the turkey section on top of the body, with the tips of the fibers pointing toward the hook eye.

6. Add some dubbing to the thread for the thorax. This dubbing can be applied rather loosely. Before dubbing the thorax, add a drop of cement on the top of the fly, to reinforce all the materials tied off there. Then dub the nymph's thorax.

7. Tie in a partridge feather by the tip. Make no more than two wraps of hackle, and then tie off the feather.

8. Divide the hackle fibers evenly, pressing them to the sides of the fly. Bring the wing case forward and tie it down.

9. Cut away the excess wing case. Shape the fly's head, tie off the thread, and add cement.

THE PALE MORNING DUN NYMPH

On this pattern, an imitation of an important mayfly nymph, the wing case is made from a feather taken from the flank of a mallard, rather than a section of a goose or turkey wing quill. You can also use a wood-duck flank feather. Since this is a small nymph, pick a flank feather that's darker and smaller than most.

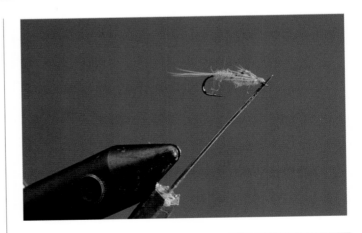

The Pale Morning Dun Nymph

Hook:	1X- or 2X-long wet-fly hook, size 14 or 16.
Thread:	Light brown 8/0.
Tail:	Ginger hackle fibers.
Rib:	Extra-fine silver wire.
Abdomen:	Pale yellow wool dubbing (you can add some sparkle if you like).
Wing case:	Mallard or wood-duck flank feather.
Thorax:	Pale yellow wool dubbing.
Legs:	Light elk hair (or ginger hackle fibers).

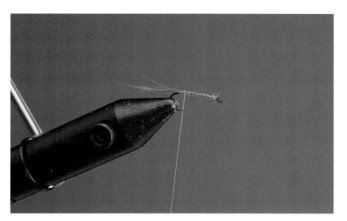

1. Attach the thread one hook-eye from the front of the shank and wrap back to just above the point. Strip a half-dozen fibers from a ginger hackle and tie them in. Bind the tail fibers all the way to the beginning of the bend, and then wind the thread forward five or six turns.

2. Tie in the ribbing wire, leaving a little space between the tail and the wire. Advance the thread to the center of the body.

3. Dub the body. Wind the dubbed thread to the rear first. Make one turn of dubbing behind the ribbing wire, then reverse direction and wrap forward. Stop dubbing one hook-eye length behind the front of the shank.

4. Wind the rib forward and tie it off. Bring the thread back to the rear of the thorax area.

5. Select a small mallard-flank feather. Strip away the fluff and some of the fibers, leaving enough to cover the top of the thorax and some of the sides. Hold the feather in place with the tip forward and the concave side up. Make three or four snug turns of thread, wrapping toward the rear of the fly. Gently pull on the feather to draw the tips of the fibers under the thread wraps.

6. Make another few wraps to the rear, until you reach the center of the hook, and then advance the thread to the middle of the thorax area. Add a drop of cement to the wraps. Twist some dubbing onto the thread (it can be a little looser than the dubbing for the abdomen) and make the fly's thorax.

7. Clip a few elk hairs and tie them on top, with the tips pointing rearward. The hair should reach just beyond the wing case.

8. Divide the hairs into two clumps with your thumb-nail.

9. Fold the wing case over the thorax and tie it down. As you tie the case down, lift up on the butt of the feather to keep it centered on top of the hook.

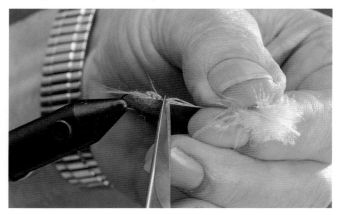

10. Cut away the butt end of the wing case and finish shaping the head.

11. Tie off the thread and apply a drop of cement.

THE BLUE-WINGED OLIVE NYMPH

In many trout streams, blue-winged olives are among the most abundant mayflies, and patterns that imitate them are very important to fly fishers. This fly represents the nymph. The techniques used in tying it are mostly the same as those employed in the previous fly, the Pale Morning Dun, except for the tails and wing case. On the Blue-Winged Olive Nymph, we'll make the tail with three moose-body hairs. The wing case is made of raffia, a type of grass. You can buy raffia in a lot of colors, or purchase white or cream material and dye it whatever color you need. I like raffia for wing cases because it looks very natural.

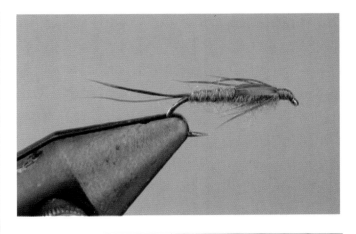

The Blue-Winged Olive Nymph

Hook:	1X- or 2X-long wet-fly hook, sizes 14 to 18.
Thread:	Olive brown 8/0.
Tail:	Three moose-body hairs.
Rib:	Extra-fine copper wire.
Abdomen:	Olive brown wool dubbing.
Wing case:	Dark brown raffia.
Thorax:	Olive brown wool dubbing.
Legs:	Moose-body hair (or wood-duck fibers).

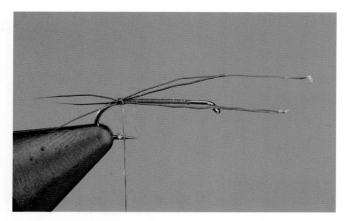

1. Attach the thread and wind it back to the end of the shank. Cut three moose-body hairs and align their tips. Tie in the hairs; the tails should be almost as long as the hook shank.

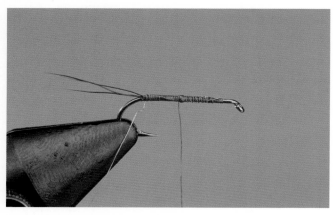

2. Bind down the butts of the tails, then wind back to the end of the shank. Bring the thread behind the hook and under the tails, so that you make a wrap around the hook right under the base of the tails. This wrap behind and under the tails will make the hairs spread out. After spreading the tails, tie in the wire for the rib.

3. Dub the nymph's body. Wind the rib forward and tie it off.

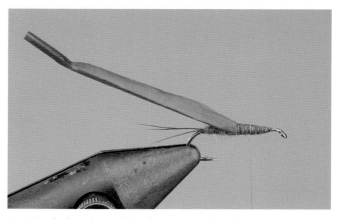

4. Wind the thread back to roughly the center of the body. Tie in a strip of raffia. Use a piece wide enough so that it will cover the top of the thorax.

5. Dub the fly's thorax. This dubbing can be a little looser than that used for the abdomen.

6. Tie in six moose hairs for the legs. The tips of the hairs should reach a little beyond the wing case.

7. Divide the hairs, three to each side. Pull the wing case over the top of the thorax and tie it down. Make the first tie-down wrap with very little tension, then lift the end of the raffia and tighten the wrap. Make another couple of wraps while pulling up on the piece of raffia. This makes the wing case narrow at the front, just like one on a real nymph. Cut the excess raffia, finish the fly's head, and apply cement.

THE GOLDEN STONEFLY NYMPH

I came up with this design while fishing the Bighorn River in Montana, which has an abundance of these insects. Like many stonefly patterns, this one has double wing cases made of folded pieces of a wing quill. We'll attach the tails on top of a layer of dubbing, a trick that automatically separates them and makes them more realistic.

The Golden Stonefly Nymph

Hook:	Tiemco 200R, size 8 or 10.
Thread:	Orange 8/0.
Abdomen:	A mix of golden yellow and orange wool.
Tail:	Golden orange turkey biots.
Rib:	Fine copper wire.
Wing cases:	Sections from a light turkey wing quill.
Thorax:	A mix of golden yellow and orange wool.
Legs:	Elk mane.

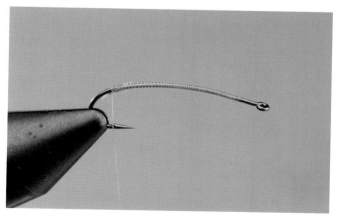

1. Attach the thread one hook-eye length behind the eye. Cover the hook shank with thread wraps, stopping just above the barb.

2. Shape the underbody with wool dubbing.

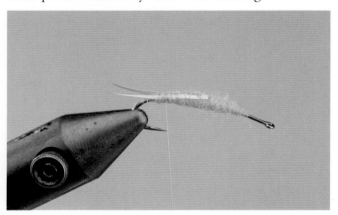

3. Tie in the tails on top of the dubbing. Attaching them this way guarantees that the tails will be separated.

4. Tie in the ribbing wire.

5. Add a thin layer of dubbing to cover the thread wraps and other materials. Stop about a third of the way from the front of the shank.

6. Wind the rib to the front of the abdomen and tie it off.

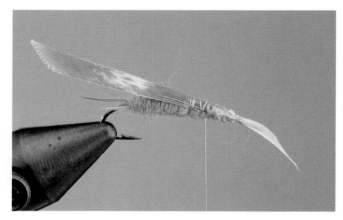

7. Add a piece of turkey quill for the first wing case.

8. Dub the nymph's thorax, making it fatter than the abdomen.

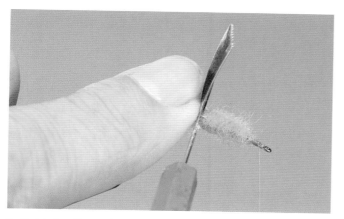

9. Fold the first wing case over your bodkin.

10. Tie down the first wing case and cut off the excess material.

11. Attach the quill section for the second wing case.

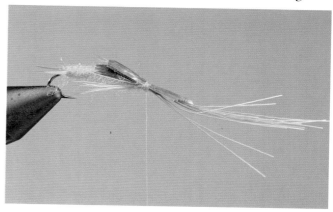

12. Tie in the legs and divide them, pushing an equal number to each side. Fold the second wing case over your bodkin and tie it down. The second case is folded slightly forward of the fold in the first one.

13. Trim the excess wing case and the butts of the legs. Finish the nymph's head, half-hitch the thread, and add a drop of cement.

THE PHEASANT TAIL NYMPH

You can't write a fly-tying book and not include this nymph. The Pheasant Tail can represent nearly all of the smaller mayflies. My version is a bit different from the standard pattern. For one thing, I use wool dubbing as an underbody to give the fly a better shape. The wing case on my Pheasant Tail is made of raffia, and the thorax is wool dubbing, neither of which is used on the original version. What doesn't change is the fly's versatility. Tie this fly with various colors of pheasant tail fibers and wire ribs to imitate many types of small mayflies.

The Pheasant Tail Nymph

Hook:	Tiemco 200R, sizes 12 through 18.
Thread:	Black 8/0.
Underbody:	Gray or tan wool dubbing.
Rib:	Extra-fine wire.
Tails:	The tips of several pheasant tail fibers.
Abdomen:	Pheasant-tail fibers.
Wing case:	Brown raffia.
Legs:	Moose-body hair.

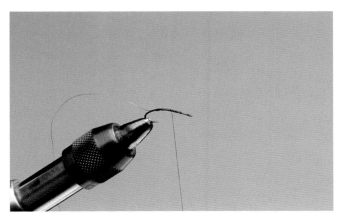

1. Wrap a layer of thread on the hook shank. Attach the ribbing wire.

2. Make a tapered, slender underbody with wool dubbing.

3. Wind the thread to the rear of the shank. Strip several fibers from a pheasant tail. Hold the fibers above the rear of the hook and measure the length of the tail. The tail should be as long as the hook gap is wide.

4. Tie the tips of the fibers to the hook with a few snug wraps. Leave the butts of the fibers intact; you will use them to make the body.

5. Advance the thread. Use counterclockwise wraps when applying the pheasant tail fibers. Wrap the body with the pheasant tail fibers. Tie off the pheasant fibers, and bring the thread back to about the middle of the hook shank.

6. Wind the rib forward and tie it off.

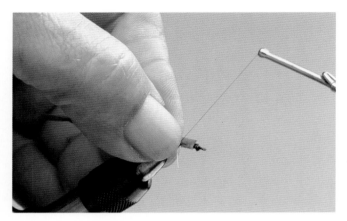

7. Tie on a strip of raffia for the wing case.

8. Dub the thorax. Make it fatter than the abdomen.

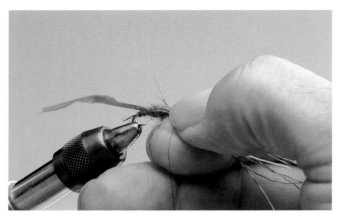

9. Tie a half-dozen moose hairs on top. Divide the hairs into two equal bunches, and push them down along the sides of the thorax.

10. Pull the wing case over the thorax and tie it down. Cut off all the excess material and finish the nymph's head.

CHAPTER 5

Tying Streamers

The term "streamer" takes in a lot of territory. Many streamers are large, attractor-style wet flies tied on long-shank hooks. Others are tied to resemble specific types of baitfish or fry. Tying streamers involves most of the skills you've already learned, along with a few new tricks, such as making the deer-hair head of a Muddler Minnow. Since they're generally larger than dry flies, wets, or nymphs, streamers provide a lot of room for creativity. The Toothpick Fry, for instance, will show you how to use a piece of a toothpick to shape the body of a fly. First, let's look at a type of streamer originally tied to represent not a minnow, but a leech.

STRIP FLIES

I had been an instructor at Gary Borger's fly-fishing schools for five or six years before I showed him any of my flies. That changed after the conclusion of one of his schools. It was customary for the instructors to gather after class to fish in the casting ponds. The ponds were filled with some very nice fish for the students to sharpen their skills on. Catch and release was always the order of the day. That's why the fish were as big as they

were. And I think it probably had something to do with why they were as selective as any I had ever fished over.

I decided to tie on a fly I had developed years earlier for just such difficult situations. I called it the Strip Fly. Little did I know that the fly would soon become known to anglers everywhere.

Gary walked over to me while I was landing a particularly nice fish, and watched as I removed the fly and returned the fish to the water.

"What the heck do you call that fly?" he asked.

"The Strip Fly," I answered. I told him that I tied it as a nymph, a leech, and as a streamer, and had great success all three ways.

Gary liked the idea and used the nymph and leech versions himself. When he wrote his book *Naturals*, he described the pattern. It wasn't long before strip patterns with various names hit the market. Most of them used a strip of rabbit fur in place of the muskrat strip I used on my flies.

Today, anglers are tying fur-strip patterns for many different species of fish. Trout, bass, pike, muskies, and a lot of other fish all take these flies. Let's see how a couple of them are made.

THE ORIGINAL STRIP FLY

I first tied this style of fly as a leech pattern. The tanned muskrat strip used for the wing has a lot of action in the water. Later, I devised a Muddler version and even a Strip Fly tied as a nymph. Here's the original pattern.

The Original Strip Fly

Hook:	2X- or 3X-long nymph or streamer hook, your choice of size.
Thread:	Black 8/0.
Body:	Flat silver tinsel.
Wing:	A strip of tanned muskrat hide as long as the hook shank.
Hackle:	Grizzly.

It's an easy fly to tie. From a tanned muskrat hide, cut a strip about as long as the hook. Cut the piece in the shape of a pennant; the tapered end will go to the rear of the fly. Wrap a tinsel body on the hook. Tie in the muskrat strip by the thicker end. Wind a conical hackle collar as you would on a wet fly, and cement the fly's head. That's it.

The Original Strip Fly.

THE STRIP LEECH

This is a longer, slightly fancier version of a Strip Fly. It uses a strip of rabbit hide instead of muskrat. Most fly shops carry rabbit strips, saving you the trouble of cutting your own. Use your imagination when you tie these flies. By changing the colors of the materials, you can make Strip Leeches represent all sorts of baitfish as well as leeches. The following is a pattern I've found very effective.

The Strip Leech

Hook:	4X-long streamer hook, your choice of size.
Thread:	Orange 3/0.
Wing:	Black rabbit strip.
Rib:	Copper wire.
Body:	Golden amber (not quite orange) wool dubbing, with some sparkle added.
Hackle:	Dyed-red golden pheasant breast feather.

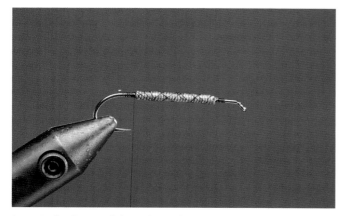

1. Wind a base of thread on the hook shank. If you want a weighted leech (and you usually do), wrap the hook with lead wire. Spiral the thread back and forth over the weighting wire, and coat the wire and thread wraps with cement.

2. Separate the hairs where you are going to tie the strip to the hook shank. Tie the rabbit strip at the bend of the hook with a couple of tight wraps. Leave a couple of inches of the strip hanging off the rear of the hook; you can cut it to whatever length you want after completing the fly. Lift the strip and make two tight wraps right in front of the skin. This locks the strip in place. Attach the wire for the rib, leaving room behind it for one wrap of dubbed thread, and advance the thread to the middle of the hook.

3. Prepare a large batch of wool dubbing with some sparkle yarn mixed in. Tease quite a bit of the dubbing from your carding brushes. For a size 4, 4X-long hook, you will need a skein of dubbing about five inches long. Dub the fly's body, beginning at the center. Wind the dubbing back to the ribbing wire, make one wrap between the wire and the tie-in spot of the rabbit strip, and then wrap forward. Stop the body about two hook-eye lengths from the front of the shank. Wind the rib and tie it off.

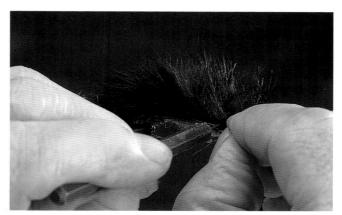

4. Pull the rabbit strip over the top of the body. Separate the hairs at the tie-in spot.

5. Grasp the strip close to the hook eye with your right hand and pull it tight. Pass the bobbin over the top of the strip and position the thread at the tie-in spot. Pull the thread tight. You can now let go of the strip at the hook eye, as long as you keep the thread tight. Make a few more tight wraps in the same spot. Lift the front of the strip and make two tight wraps of thread around the hook shank only, and then another couple of wraps around the rabbit strip. This locks the strip to the hook.

6. Cut the excess part of the strip. Bind down the little piece of hide where you cut the strip. Add a little cement to the wraps.

7. Tie in the hackle feather by the tip.

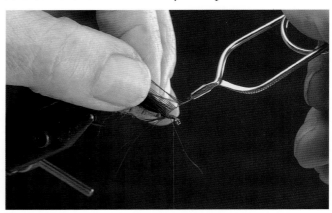

8. Wrap the hackle, folding the fibers to the rear as you do. Make as many turns as you can; usually, two or three wraps are all you can get.

9. Shape the head, tie off the thread, and add cement.

WHEN IN ALASKA, TAKE A TOOTHPICK

I awoke to an Alaskan morning full of anticipation. Today I would catch some of the big, powerful trout Alaska is known for. We loaded our gear and headed for the river. The depth of the water demanded heavy flies and a lot of lead. Not my kind of fishing; it's too damned much work. I sat with the guide and talked fishing and other such important matters while my partners chucked lead and fished deep. Suddenly, there was a loud splash close to us. I thought a fish had come up for an insect, but the guide pointed out that the salmon fry were migrating and that the shallows were full of them. The trout that had made the splash was probably chasing fry at the surface, he explained.

At the mention of "fry," I immediately reached for a fly box containing a Toothpick Fry. The guide looked dubiously at it. He didn't think I would catch anything if I didn't fish deep like everyone else. Some people just don't like change, I guess. But I like being different, so I tied on the Toothpick Fry and prepared to show him just how wrong he was.

The fish had risen just downstream from me. I needed to drop the fly to the side so that I could swing it in front of where the fish rose. I made the cast and held my rod high to keep as much line off the water as possible. The fly cut a V in the water as it swung into position. A huge splash convinced the guide that old dogs could teach him a new trick. The big rainbow that had eaten the fly was photo-worthy and, after having its picture taken, was released unharmed. The Toothpick Fry took three more equally nice fish, each on the first cast.

This unconventional baitfish fly isn't just for Alaskan fishing. It will work wherever trout eat fry or small minnows, and that's almost everywhere.

The Toothpick Fry

Hook:	Daiichi 1580, size 6 or 8.
Thread:	White 3/0 Monocord.
Back and tail:	Beige sparkle yarn.
Underbody:	A piece of a toothpick and pearlescent Mylar tubing.
Body:	Pearlescent Mylar tinsel.
Head:	Built up with the tying thread, with dots of black lacquer for eyes.
Throat (optional):	Red hackle fibers.

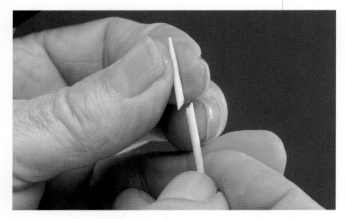

1. Cut the end off a toothpick at an angle. The piece you cut should be as long as the shank of the hook.

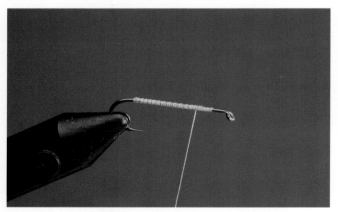

2. Wrap the hook shank with two layers of thread, stopping a little behind the eye.

3. Attach the toothpick with the angled end at the front. When you tie the toothpick in place, spin the bobbin counterclockwise (as viewed from above) to take the twist out of the thread. This lets the thread flatten as you wrap it around the toothpick, making for a smooth foundation.

4. Bind the toothpick to the hook with several layers of thread, making a smooth, tapered shape. Finish with the thread hanging over the barb of the hook.

5. Tie on the sparkle yarn at the rear of the hook. Hold the yarn in place on top of the toothpick, and wrap the thread forward to bind down the yarn. Then wind the thread back to the rear of the hook.

6. Cut a piece of medium-size Mylar tubing a little longer than the hook shank. Remove the cotton core from the tubing. Fray one end of the tubing by rolling it between your fingers, and slide the tubing over the hook shank with the frayed end to the rear. The frayed section extends beyond the tying thread.

7. Gather the strands of frayed Mylar tubing behind the bend of the hook, and make a few wraps of thread to bind the tubing to the hook. At the same place, attach enough flat Mylar tinsel to cover the entire body. Secure the thread with half hitches, and cut it. Try to keep the band of thread at the rear of the fly as narrow and neat as possible.

8. Push the Mylar tubing rearward and attach the thread to the hook right behind the eye. Unravel just enough of the tubing so that the thread can slip between the strands. Gather the strands in front of the hook eye, pull the tubing tight, and make a few wraps of thread to bind it to the hook. Wrap the flat tinsel forward over the entire underbody, and secure it at the front of the hook.

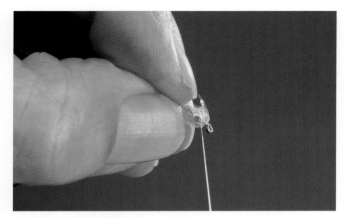

9. Shape the head of the fly. Fold the ends of the frayed tubing to the rear and wrap over them with thread. You want to build up a fairly large head. If you want the fly to have a red throat, tie in a clump of red hackle fibers now.

11. Apply small drops of black lacquer to make eyes. The end of a toothpick makes a good applicator.

10. After building up the head, half-hitch the thread and cut it away. You want to end up with a shape like that of a small minnow. Coat the head and body with a plastic cement and let the fly dry overnight.

12. After the eyes have dried, coat the head with cement. If you haven't done so already, trim the tail to length.

MUDDLER MINNOWS

Most anglers agree that Muddler Minnows are among the best streamers. Tying Muddlers uses a number of techniques, but the one that probably gives beginners the most trouble is making the deer-hair head. I'll show you two ways, one of which avoids having to trim the fly's head to shape.

I use mule-deer hair for the Muddler's collar and head. Mule deer flares and spins more easily than white-tailed deer because the mule-deer fibers are thicker and have a greater volume of air inside them. Here's the parts list for how I tie Muddlers.

Muddler Minnow

Hook:	2X- or 3X-long, sizes 4 through 14.
Thread:	Black 3/0.
Tail:	Mottled turkey quill sections.
Rib:	Fine, oval gold tinsel.
Body:	Medium flat silver tinsel.
Underwing:	Squirrel tail.
Wing:	Mottled turkey quill sections.
Collar and head:	Mule-deer body hair.

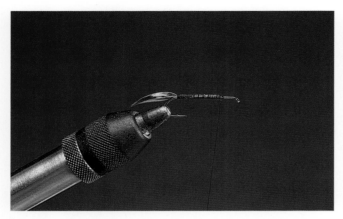

1. Attach the thread about a quarter of the way back on the hook shank and wrap back to right above the barb. Cut narrow slips from matched turkey quills. Tie in the quill sections for the tail. Bind the butts along the hook shank to make a smooth foundation for the body.

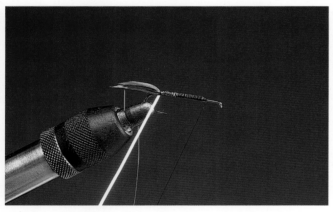

2. Cut a piece of oval tinsel, and strip some of the metallic covering from one end to expose the tinsel's core. Tie the core to the bottom of the hook shank, leaving room between the oval tinsel and the base of the tail for one turn of the flat tinsel. After attaching the oval tinsel, tie in a piece of flat tinsel.

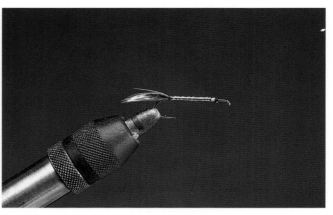

3. Wind the body and the rib. Secure both pieces of tinsel and trim the excess. Make several wraps of thread in front of the body to create a base for the wing.

4. Cut a small clump of hair from a squirrel tail. Cut the hair to length, add a drop of cement to the tie-in spot, and tie the hair in place.

5. Select a matching pair of turkey quills (one from a left wing and one from a right wing), and cut a section from the wider part of each feather. Put the two quill sections together with the shinier sides facing each other and the tips aligned. Stroke the tops of the quill sections to give the pieces a slight downward curve; this is called "humping." Cut the quill sections to length and tie them in place.

6. We'll tie our first Muddler with the no-trim head technique. Cut a clump of mule-deer hair. The amount of hair varies according to the size of the hook. For now, use a clump about the thickness of an ordinary pencil. Stack the hair to even the tips. Remove the hair from the stacker and hold it in your right hand. Measure the length of the collar. The tips of the collar should reach about halfway back on the hook shank.

7. Transfer the hair to your left hand, marking the tie-in spot with your thumbnail. Cut the hair slightly in front of your thumbnail. Exactly where to cut the hair depends on the size of the fly. If you're tying on a size 10 hook, cut the hair $1/16$ of an inch in front of your nail; on a larger fly, cut it farther away. The butts sticking out beyond your fingertips will become the head of your Muddler.

8. Hold the butt ends of the hair at the rear of the hook eye. Make one wrap around the hook shank and hair at the front of your thumbnail.

9. Flare the hair just a little by pulling on the bobbin. Now make a second wrap around the hair and hook shank. With the bobbin below the hook, start to pull directly downward. Do not pull at an angle and do not tip the hair at an angle. As you apply the downward pressure, gradually release the hair from your left index finger and thumb.

11. To taper the head, make a couple of angled turns of thread through the hair and toward the front. Make these wraps with less tension on the thread.

10. Completely release your grip on the hair while continuing to tighten the thread. Once the thread is tight and the hair stops spinning, start to push the hair around the hook shank until it is evenly distributed. Keep the thread tight and make another couple of wraps in the same spot.

12. When you reach the back of the hook eye, make a wrap or two, and then tie off the thread. You will have produced a nicely shaped Muddler head that requires no trimming.

A TRIMMED MUDDLER HEAD

Some anglers want a slightly longer, denser head on a Muddler Minnow. And some tiers prefer to trim the head to a certain shape. To make a trimmed head, use two clumps of hair, spinning one around the hook and then spinning the second in front of the first. Here's how to do it.

1. Construct the tail, body, and wing as you did on the first Muddler. Cut a clump of mule-deer hair, and spin and push it around the hook. Don't worry about the length of the butts, because you will trim them later. Once the hair is tight, pull the butts to the rear and make a wrap of thread in front of the hair. Push the hair as much to the rear as you can. Then cut a second clump of hair and hold it in front of the first bundle, as shown here.

2. Spin and push the second bundle of hair around the hook. Once the hair is distributed evenly around the shank, pull all of it to the rear and make a couple of snug wraps around the shank behind the eye of the hook. Half-hitch the thread and cut it. Cement the half hitch.

4. You want to produce an even, tapered shape like this. Compare this with the no-trim head, and you'll see that this one is a little longer and denser.

3. When you trim the head, start on the bottom. Once you've trimmed the bottom, shape the rest of the head. With a little practice, you should be able to trim a Muddler with about a dozen snips. If the collar is a little fuller than you like, just trim off a few hairs with a double-edged razor.

Here's one more Muddler trick. Remember the Strip Flies at the start of this chapter? If you leave a little extra room at the front of a Strip Fly, you can add a Muddler head. A Strip Muddler is an effective, durable streamer that represents a sculpin or some other baitfish.

THE GOLDEN SQUIRREL

It seems fitting to end this book with the first pattern that I designed, the Golden Squirrel. This pattern has become my signature fly, and one that I often tie at shows. It's as productive as it is handsome, and I think you'll enjoy tying and using it. Since the Golden Squirrel is a simple fly that uses techniques you've already learned, I think a photo and pattern will suffice.

The Golden Squirrel	
Hook:	2X-long hook, such as a Mustad 94831 dry fly hook, size 10.
Thread:	Black 8/0.
Tail:	Red hackle fibers.
Body:	Flat gold tinsel.
Wing:	Hair from the tail of a red or fox squirrel.
Cheeks:	Jungle cock.

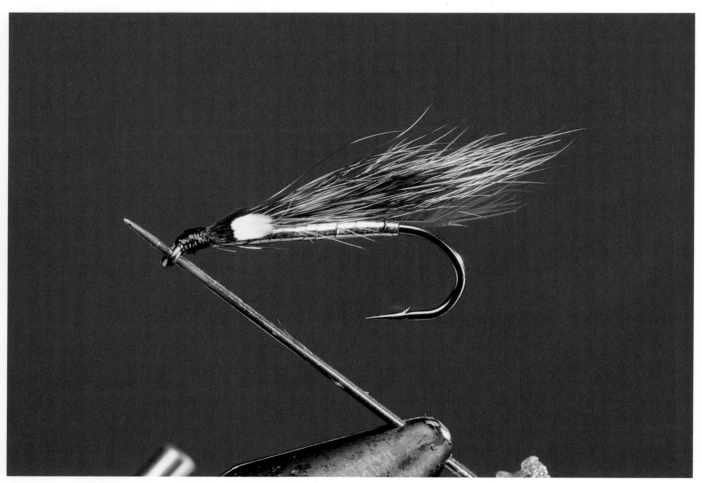

The Golden Squirrel.